Prayers to Move Your Mountains

REGENCY PUBLISHING HOUSE
NASHVILLE / NEW YORK

Published in Nashville, Tennessee, by Thomas Nelson, Inc.

Library of Congress Cataloging-in-Publication Data

ISBN 0-7852-6864-2

Printed in the United States of America

1 2 3 4 5 6 BVG 05 04 03 02 01 00

CONTENTS

INTRODUCTION

Only God can move mountains, but faith and prayer move God.
—E. M. Bounds[1]

A small congregation in the Appalachians received a choice piece of land willed to them by a deceased church member. Scraping together together their limited resources, the people pooled enough money together to build a beautiful new sanctuary. Ten days before the new church was to be dedicated, the local building inspector approached the pastor. "Reverend, I'm sorry but your parking lot is too small in proportion to the size of your building. I'm afraid until you double the size of your parking lot, the city cannot allow you to use your new sanctuary."

"But sir," the pastor responded, "we have no more room to expand. Every square inch of land is utilized except for this hill that stands directly behind the church. Our people just don't have the money to level this hill and then have it paved."

"I'm sorry," the inspector repeated, "but I'm just following city regulations. Unless you do something to move this mountain out of the way and put in more parking spaces, you cannot use your sanctuary."

Undaunted, the next Sunday morning the pastor explained the church's dilemma and then announced, "Tonight, there's going to be a special prayer service. We're going to ask God to remove this mountain behind our church and somehow provide enough money to have it paved and painted in time for the dedication service next week. But I only want people with mountain-moving faith to come."

That evening, twenty-four of the congregation's three hundred members assembled for prayer. For nearly three hours they sought God, asking for His divine intervention. At ten o'clock the pastor gave the final "Amen." "We'll open next Sunday as scheduled," he assured everyone. "God has never let us down before, and I believe He will be faithful this time as well."

Monday morning as he was working in his study, the pastor heard a loud knock at his door. "Come in," he called out from behind his desk. The door opened and in walked a rough-looking construction foreman who removed his hard hat as he entered.

"Excuse me, Reverend. I'm from a construction company over in the next county. We're building a new shopping mall and we need some fill dirt. Would you be willing to sell us a chunk of that mountain behind your church? We'll pay you for the dirt we remove and pave all the exposed area free of charge, if we can have it right away. We're at a standstill until we get the dirt in and allow it to settle properly."

The next Sunday the church was dedicated as originally planned. There were far more members with "mountain-moving faith" on opening Sunday than there had been the previous week!

EVERYONE HAS A MOUNTAIN TO CLIMB

Mountains—like people and snowflakes—express themselves in an infinite number of shapes and sizes. Fooling the senses, some appear ominous yet in reality mask what is scalable by even the most pedestrian mountain climber. Others hide behind a seemingly diminutive yet virtually impenetrable fortress.

Have you ever faced a mountain that seemed impossible to overcome? Perhaps you encountered a dilemma that required more than you could give.

The various mountains we face—difficult relationships, destructive and sinful habits, stresses that don't seem to go away—reinforce to us that we're human. Yet mountain or molehill, they cannot be overcome without the intervention of a loving heavenly Father who alone possesses the ability to scale the unscalable.

Mountains are beneficial because they serve as reminders of our *in*ability and God's *a*bility. The apostle Paul wrote that our God is "able to do exceedingly abundantly above all that we ask or think, *according to the power that works in us*." (Eph. 3:20 NKJV, italics added). Any power at our disposal comes not from the power resident *within* us, but the grace of God working *through* us.

What kind of faith would we have if we never faced any challenges? E. M. Bounds, perhaps the father of the modern prayer movement, wrote over a century ago:

> Prayer in its highest form and grandest success assumes the attitude of a wrestler with God. It is the contest, trial, and victory of faith; a victory not secured from an enemy, but from him who tries our faith that he may enlarge it: that tests our strength to make us stronger.[2]

DOES PRAYER CHANGE PEOPLE OR THINGS?

In the not too distant past, bumper stickers, refrigerator magnets, and bookmarks were emblazoned with the popular adage, "Prayer Changes Things." Not long thereafter, an assortment of prominent Christian leaders countered with a maxim of their own: "Prayer doesn't change *things*, prayer changes *people*." In other words, our prayers don't necessarily change our situation, they change us, or at least our perspective. So which one is it? Does prayer change people or does prayer change things?

Somewhere in the middle of the crossfire lies the heart of true prayer. God desires first and foremost to change the hearts of men and women. His ultimate goal is to bring glory to Himself as His kingdom spreads throughout the earth. But through the changed hearts of His people, He chooses to do His work here on earth. Through prayer. Prayer changes people, and, through changed people, prayer changes things.

Walking on the road to Jerusalem with His disciples one day, Jesus was hungry, so He stopped at a nearby fig tree. Disappointed that it didn't have any fruit, Jesus spoke to the tree, "Let no one eat fruit from you ever again" (Mark 11:14 NKJV).

The next morning, Jesus and His disciples once again walked along the same road and passed by the same tree. In only one day's time, the tree was now withered up and dead. Jesus then spoke to His now-astonished companions:

> Have faith in God. For assuredly, I say to you, whoever says to this mountain, "Be removed and be cast into the sea," and does not doubt in his heart, but believes that those things he says will be done, he will have whatever he says. Therefore I say to you, whatever things you ask when you pray, believe

> that you receive them, and you will have them.
> (Mark 11:22–24 NKJV)

Jesus chose a mountain to illustrate the awesome power of prayer. Especially in the days before bulldozers and earthmovers, mountains symbolized the immovable. Mountains exemplified anything so ominous in a person's life that it couldn't be removed apart from the power of God. And that is the power Jesus gave to His church through the Holy Spirit.

Pride, lust, an unsaved spouse, a broken relationship—all function as mountains in the lives of ordinary people. Some mountains are self-inflicted; others are inflicted upon us. Regardless, we all have mountains to climb. Fortunately, God doesn't leave us alone on the side of those mountains to be buffeted by the gale-force winds they present.

MOUNTAINS, PROBLEMS, AND THE PRESENCE OF GOD

Throughout the Bible, mountains have symbolized not only problems, but also the place where people encounter God's life-giving presence.

Had an angel of the Lord not stopped him, Abraham would have offered his son, Isaac, as a sacrifice on the side of Mt. Moriah (Gen. 22). Moses encountered the burning bush and received the Ten Commandments on Mt. Sinai (Ex. 19). The Temple, the center of Jewish worship, was built on Mt. Zion. The surrounding nations, understanding the connection, referred to Israel's God as the *God of the hills* (1 Kings 20:28).

In Jesus' life, the mountain was both a place of temptation where His humanity was tested (Matt. 4:8) and the transfiguration where His divinity was revealed (Matt. 17:1–2). Last of all, we look forward to the day when the mountain of the Lord's temple is raised up for all the earth to see and where all the earth's inhabitants will gather (Isa. 2:2; Mic. 4:1).

So mountains operate as the location where both our problems and God's presence meet. And oddly enough, the two are related. Our problems *can* lead us into the presence of God. The temptations we face *can* lead us into Jesus' transfiguring presence, that is, when we go to Him in prayer.

Our desire is that you will encounter the presence of God in the midst of your problems. That in the middle of your temptations you would experience Jesus transfigured in your life. And that this book would play a pivotal role in bridging your problems and temptations with Jesus' transfiguring presence.

That we should pray because it is important isn't an issue for most Christians. We all realize that prayer is essential to growing in our relationship with Jesus Christ and that, in some way, prayer makes a difference. It's the *hows* and *whats* of prayer that seem to keep us from doing what we really know we should do. And what we want to do.

Ask people to describe the biggest hurdles they face in prayer, and you will probably hear one of two answers: (1) "I just don't have the motivation and commitment to make it a vital part of my life"; and (2) "I'd pray longer, but after five or ten minutes, I don't know what to say."

But if you knew that your prayers would really make a difference in your life and the lives of others, would you be more inclined to pray? Of course. Almost anybody would.

Although we place no guarantees that the prayers in this book will bring results, we hope they will provide a model, a launching pad, for catapulting *your* prayers into the heavens.

HOW THIS BOOK ON PRAYER IS DIFFERENT THAN ANY OTHER

Since the book of Psalms' inception, the church has used written prayers to approach the throne of grace. Today, many Christian traditions and practices utilize prayer books such as *The Book of Common Prayer.* Prayer books are legion. So why one more prayer book?

What separates this book from others lies in the fact that it empowers *your* prayer life. Each section walks you through the discipline of prayer, with the hope of guiding you toward praying effectively. This book leads you through the important components: preparation, confession of sin, personal requests, and praying for the issues on God's heart.

The tendency for many of us is to focus only on our needs or God's. But the two aren't mutually exclusive. When we focus only on our needs, we gravitate into selfish belief. When we focus only on God's needs, we miss the connection that God cares about our needs as well.

Our goal is that when you pick up your Bible to spend time with God, you will include this book. Not because it is a crutch to lean on, but because it serves as a helpful aid in drawing you through prayer. In fact, we believe this book will motivate you to pray more.

For example, as you pray, you can begin by telling God what His love means to you (Chapter 1-3. Cherishing God's Love). Moving ahead, you can thank Him for what He's already done in sending Jesus to die on the cross for your sins (Chapter 2-3. Thanking God for the Cross and the Blood). As you draw closer into God's presence, share with Him your desire to grow deeper in purity (Chapter 3-1. Guarding Purity). Follow that prayer by seeking forgiveness of sin from selfishness (Chapter 4-13. Dying to Selfishness). As you move into areas of personal requests, you can bring a particularly anxious situation from work before the throne of God (Chapter 5-2. Peace for Worry). Bringing your time of prayer to a conclusion, you can ask for God to give you His heart for the less fortunate (Chapter 11-3. Compassion for the Poor and Needy).

Because effectual prayer is led by the Spirit, it should vary each time you pray. Sometimes your prayer will focus mainly on the character and attributes of God. Sometimes God will spend the majority of the time doing a cleansing work in your life. Or you may find yourself focusing on the kingdom of God. Yet at other times, you will find your prayer time concentrating on specific needs in your life or the lives of others. The key is to remain sensitive to the leading of the Holy Spirit as you pray.

Most important, don't limit yourself to the words printed in this book. Allow them to launch you deeper into prayer that is led by the Holy Spirit.

Through the prayers in this book, may you discover the power to move mountains in your life and for the cause of Jesus Christ.

Michael J. Klassen
Thomas M. Frieling

1

WORSHIPING GOD FOR WHO HE IS

To worship means to attribute worth. When we worship, we attribute to God His "worth-ship." In other words, we tell Him how much He means to us. Worship focuses on *who* God is—His inherent attributes and character. Worship ascribes to God His power to intervene on our behalf, His love for us by sending Jesus, or His wisdom in determining the course of our lives.

God created us for the express purpose of worshiping Him. In Isaiah 43:21 God described the righteous as, "the people whom I formed for myself so that they might declare my praise" (NRSV). The Westminster Catechism put it into layman's terms: "Man's chief end is to glorify God, and to enjoy Him forever."[1] Worship, then, is a matter of glorifying and enjoying God.

When we attribute to God His worth, we begin tapping into our very reason for being. In fact, taking our fleshly nature out of the equation, we find that worship comes naturally. As we enjoy God, He in turn enjoys us. It's no wonder that we sense the presence of God as we worship Him!

Our worship and praise literally builds a throne for our heavenly

Father to reign on. In Psalm 22:3 King David prayed, "But You are holy, Enthroned in the praises of Israel" (NKJV). By exalting God, we welcome His real and manifest presence into our daily situations. Doing so releases His power and character into our lives.

Beginning prayer in worship brings God's perspective. When the psalmist became discouraged by the apparent success of the wicked and lack of it among the righteous, he brought his concerns before the Father. Watch what happened then:

> When I thought how to understand this,
> It was too painful for me—
> *Until I went into the sanctuary of God,*
> *Then I understood their end.* (Ps. 73:16–17 NKJV, italics added)

Until he entered the sanctuary—the presence of God—the psalmist was downcast. But everything changed when he began seeing through God's eyes.

The presence of God—which we enter into through praise and worship—draws us into God's perspective. As we see our requests from God's vantage point, they can't help but change, becoming conformed to His will. Ultimately, our prayers will be answered because, as Jesus said, "If you abide in Me, and My words abide in you, you will ask what you desire, and it shall be done for you" (John 15:7 NKJV). Abiding in Jesus—spending time with Him and enjoying Him—is a key to prayer that moves mountains.

Last of all, worship is more than a lead-in time for prayer or the songs we sing before hearing a sermon on Sunday morning. Worship is an attitude, a lifestyle. Paul wrote in 1 Corinthians 10:31, "Therefore, whether you eat or drink, or whatever you do, do all to the glory of God" NKJV. As we walk in worship, we become channels of God's presence and power, affecting everyone around us.

1

MAGNIFYING THE LORD

I will bless the LORD at all times;
His praise shall continually *be* in my mouth.
My soul shall make its boast in the LORD;
The humble shall hear of it and be glad.
Oh, magnify the LORD with me,
And let us exalt His name together.
I sought the LORD, and He heard me,
And delivered me from all my fears.
(Ps. 34:1–4 NKJV)

This day, O God, I choose to bless Your name. I bless You because You are great and Your greatness does not depend upon my circumstances. The problems of this world are mere child's play in comparison to Your ability to overcome. So I choose to focus on the Problem Solver rather than any problem. I will boast in You, O God, because nothing is impossible for You (Matt. 17:20). Only You can make the impossible possible.

I proclaim Your name, O Lord. I ascribe greatness to You, my God, for You are the Rock. Your work is perfect and *all* Your ways are just (Deut. 32:3–4). For this reason, I place my trust in You with confidence. You are greater than my problems; greater than my sins; greater than my sickness; greater than those who oppose me; greater than the powers of darkness; greater than my own shortcomings; greater than the failings of your people; greater than the powers of human government; greater than my limited conceptions of how big You really are. My God *You are* greater!

My power to overcome any situation comes only from You because greater is He who is in me than he who is in the world (1 John 4:4). My heart's desire is that Your great name will be made known throughout the earth beginning in my life.

I lift my arms in surrender to the One who reigns above the heavens and the earth. There is no power on earth greater than Yours. No love stronger. No wisdom deeper. You alone stand above the earth, but You have willingly chosen to also stand beside me.

The fact that You are great yet You choose to reveal Yourself to me through Your Son, Jesus, through Your Word, and through Your Holy Spirit, drives me to my knees in gratitude. You didn't have to reveal Yourself to me, but You did. Now may Your greatness be revealed in my life so that others may see Your glory as well (Ezek. 38:23).

See also:

1-2. Meditating on His Omnipotence and Omnipresence
2-8. Thanking God for Supplying my Needs
3-9. Building Faith and Trust
4. Sin
5-2. Peace for Worry
10. Sickness and Disease
11. Bringing in the Kingdom of God

2

MEDITATING ON HIS OMNIPOTENCE AND OMNIPRESENCE

And I heard, as it were, the voice of a great multitude, as the sound of many waters and as the sound of mighty thunderings, saying, "Alleluia! For the Lord God Omnipotent reigns!" (Rev. 19:6 NKJV)

Hallelujah! For the Lord God almighty reigns! Again I will say: Hallelujah! For the Lord God almighty reigns! The heavens and the earth are no match for Your awesome power and might. As You spoke through Your prophet Jeremiah, "Behold, I am the LORD, the God of all flesh. Is there anything too hard for Me?"(Jer. 32:27 NKJV). There is no mountain too great that Your might cannot cast it into the deepest sea. Nothing is too hard for You. I take pleasure in acknowledging my weaknesses because I know that in my weakness You are made strong (2 Cor. 12:9–10).

Despite Your great power, I have nothing to fear. I revere Your great name, but I need not be afraid of You because Your love is as great as Your power.

Through Your Son, Jesus, *Emmanuel*, You are "God with us" (Isa. 7:14; Matt. 1:23). Clothing Yourself in human flesh You prove Your love and willingness to meet me at the point of my need. Jesus, You are God's power and presence revealed. Only through You can I truly be freed from my bondage to sin.

My heart echoes the words of the psalmist, who wrote,

Where can I go from Your Spirit?
Or where can I flee from Your presence?
If I ascend into heaven,
You are there;
If I make my bed in hell, behold, You are there.
If I take the wings of the morning,
And dwell in the uttermost parts of the sea,
Even there Your hand shall lead me,
And Your right hand shall hold me.
(Ps. 139:7–10 NKJV)

God, where can I go to outrun Your love (Rom. 8:35)? Even if I were to escape to the farthest regions of the earth, I would find You there, waiting for me. You have positioned Yourself right beside me, carrying me, encouraging me, believing in me. At the end of my rope, when I feel all alone, Your Word promises that You are with me (Heb 13:5) and that no one can snatch me from Your hand (John 10:28–29). You are my refuge and strength, a very present help in trouble (Ps. 46:1).

And because I cannot escape Your love, I also know I can go to You in prayer. You alone have the ability to answer my requests according to Your power and might.

Only You can touch me like no one else. The presence of Your love and the power of Your word extend to my darkest secret and deepest need. Because You are everywhere, You also see into the recesses of my heart. You know my faults, failures, and foibles better than I do. Yet even in those times—when I, above all people, detest myself the most—You accept me and call me Your very own.

Because You are all-powerful, all-present, all-wise, and all-loving, I can entrust the controls of my life to You without fear of being unloved and uncared for. You are bringing together all things in heaven and earth to work according to Your divine plan: to bring glory and honor to Yourself. You have raised up Your people for the express purpose that You would show Your power in us, and that Your name would be declared in all the earth (Ex. 9:16). And so here I am Lord, willingly giving to You the praise and honor befitting only You.

See also:

1-1. Magnifying the Lord
1-4. Praising God for His Creation
1-5. Acclaiming God's Majesty and the Beauty of Holiness
2-5. Thanking God for the Resurrection of Christ
2-7. Thanking God for Sending His Spirit
3-4. Moving in the Gifts of the Spirit
3-8. Joining God in His Will
4-1. The Prayer of Salvation (Sinner's Prayer)
4-2. The Prayer of Recommitment
5-8. Courage for Fear
10. Sickness and Disease
11. Bringing in the Kingdom of God

3

CHERISHING GOD'S LOVE

> The LORD has appeared of old to me, saying:
> "Yes, I have loved you with an everlasting love;
> Therefore with lovingkindness I have drawn you."
> (Jer. 31:3 NKJV)

Heavenly Father, when was the last time I told You that I loved You? Often I get so caught up in the busyness of *my* life and the concerns of this world that I fail to stop and tell You I love You. So here I am, expressing these often-neglected words from the depths of my heart: *I love You*.

I love You because before I was even created, You loved me (1 John 4:19). When I sought to live my life apart from You, Your love remained the same—ever beckoning me back to You again (Rom. 5:8). Even when I am unlovely and seemingly unlovable, You continue to love me and accept me because Your compassions *never* fail (Lam. 3:22). When I am faithless, You promise in Your Word that You remain faithful because You cannot deny Yourself (2 Tim. 2:13). I find comfort and security in the fact that there is nothing I can do to make You love me any more or less than You already do.

Your Word tells us "Greater love has no one than this, than to lay down one's life for his friends" (John 15:13 NKJV). I love You because You call me "friend" (John 15:15) and demonstrated the full extent of your love by giving Your only Son, Jesus, to die on a cross for me (John 13:1; 1 John 4:9). Your act of compassion was not intended to separate Yourself from me, but to draw me closer to You (Heb. 10:19–20).

Your gift of salvation is too great to ever repay, but You didn't stop there. You allowed me to taste of Your sweet love (Ps. 34:8). I *have* tasted and seen that You are good.

So I declare "I am my beloved's, / And his desire is toward me" (Song 7:10 NKJV). Your invitation echoes throughout eternity, calling all people to be one with You. To be captivated by Your love. To savor Your love. And to enjoy Your love forever.

The kind of love shared between the Father, Son, and Holy Spirit is the love You desire to share with me (John 17:26). I am eternally grateful to You for creating me with the express purpose of pouring Your love into my life.

Your "lovingkindness is better than life" (Ps. 63:3 NKJV). Your love gives me life. My endless pursuits of entertainment and pleasure are poor substitutes for the God-shaped hole that only You can fill.

More than showing me love, You *are* love. You are love not for what You do, but for who You are. And in response to Your great love, I dedicate myself to living for You and loving others the way You have loved me (1 John 4:7–8).

I love Your love!

See also:

1-6. Yearning for More of Jesus
2-1. Thanking God for Sending Jesus
2-4. Thanking God for His Grace and Mercy
2-10. Thanking God for Choosing Me
3-3. Bearing the Fruit of the Spirit
3-10. Finding Contentment
11-10. The Second Coming of Christ

4

PRAISING GOD FOR HIS CREATION

He has made everything beautiful in its time. Also He has put eternity in their hearts, except that no one can find out the work that God does from beginning to end. (Eccl. 3:11 NKJV)

A baby cooing . . . a tree lifting up its branches to the sky . . . a brook babbling ever so softly, all join in universal chorus giving praise to You. Your Word proclaims, "The heavens declare the glory of God" (Ps. 19:1 NKJV). As I look around I see the unmistakable imprint of Your creative work. The beauty of the mountains were sculpted by Your hands. The lush, green fields of spring remind me of Your unlimited provision. The multicolored rainbow following a summer shower recounts Your covenant of faithfulness to every living creature (Gen. 9:16). Vivid landscapes brushed in hues of red, orange, and brown ultimately point to the hand of a Master Painter. Even the feathery blankets of snow in winter speak of the power Your blood brings, washing my sins white as snow (Isa. 1:18).

All creation points to Your character and eternal power so that no one can justifiably doubt Your existence (Rom. 1:20). Lord Jesus, You are the firstborn over all creation, and by You all things were created that are in heaven and that are on earth, visible and invisible, whether thrones or dominions or principalities or powers. All things were created through You and for You (Col. 1:16). Heavenly Father, by Your will, through the word of Your Son, Jesus, and the power of Your Holy Spirit, You created the heavens and the earth out of nothing (Gen. 1:1).

After You laid the foundations of the earth, You looked over all of creation and You not only called it good, but You called it very good (Gen. 1:31). Almighty God, it was very good because it was a reflection of Your very goodness. You make all things beautiful in their time (Eccl. 3:11).

But most amazing of all is that Your defining masterpiece is me. Me! I am created in the image of the God who reigns over the universe. I will praise You, for I am fearfully and wonderfully made (Ps. 139:14). And to the same extent that You were intimately involved in my creation is the degree in which You are present working good things in my life. The extent of Your love is too great for me to fathom.

The earth *is* Yours, O Lord, and all its fullness (Ps. 24:1). And because everything in heaven and on earth is Yours, You stand independent of any influence or danger. You alone are sovereign and the resources of heaven and earth lie at Your disposal. "Ah, Lord GOD! Behold, You have made the heavens and the earth by Your great power and outstretched arm. There is nothing too hard for You" (Jer. 32:17 NKJV).

Your handiwork here on earth is just a foretaste of what heaven will be like, so I wait in eager anticipation for the day when I will see You face-to-face and enjoy the beauty of heaven with You.

See also:

1-3. Cherishing God's Love
1-5. Acclaiming God's Majesty and the Beauty of Holiness
2-6. Thanking God for Making Me the Righteousness of God in Christ
2-10. Thanking God for Choosing Me
4-3. Overcoming Pride
5-3. Hope for Despair

5

ACCLAIMING GOD'S MAJESTY AND THE BEAUTY OF HOLINESS

> Give to the LORD the glory due His name;
> Bring an offering, and come before Him.
> Oh, worship the LORD in the beauty of holiness!
> (1 Chron. 16:29 NKJV)

O Lord, our Lord, how majestic is Your name in all the earth (Ps. 8:1 NIV)! I delight in You, the King of glory. You are strong and mighty in battle (Ps. 24:7–8), and Your kingdom is built on righteousness and justice (Ps. 89:14). You have given all authority to Your Son Jesus (Matt. 28:18), the Prince of Peace (Isa. 9:6). Jesus, I rejoice that at Your name, every knee will bow—both in heaven, on earth, and under the earth—and every tongue will confess that Jesus Christ is Lord, to the glory of God the Father (Phil. 2:10–11).

Almighty God, there is no king like *my* King. There is no god like *my* God. All the nations are but a drop in the bucket compared to Your power and might (Isa. 40:15). Your reign extends from human events and the change in seasons (Dan. 2:21) through eternity (Dan. 7:14). The powers of death, sin, and hell are no match for You. I can't help but sing and shout for my King. You reign (1 Chron. 16:31)!

To look upon Your face in all Your fullness would mean certain death (Ex. 33:20). Yet You allow me—laden with sin that I am—to enter into Your presence through the blood of Jesus Christ (Heb. 4:16). And as I approach Your throne, I am enamored with Your beauty. The grandeur and splendor of Your presence astounds me.

My heart trembles at the thought that I am privileged to enter into the courts of the almighty God who reigns above the heavens and holds the destiny of earthly kingdoms in His hands (Dan. 2:21). So I build a throne of worship and praise for You to take Your rightful place (Ps. 22:3)—in my hardships (James 1:2); in my successes (Ps. 115:1); in my thoughts (Col. 3:2); in everything I do (1 Thess. 5:16–18).

Your holiness describes Your beauty. You are perfect in all Your ways (Deut. 32:4), devoid of all evil (Ps. 5:4), and unrighteousness (Ps. 92:15). There is no one like You (Isa. 40:25). Jesus, You are the manifestation of God's beauty (Isa. 4:2). The beauty of this world reflects the essence of who You are. Lord, let Your beauty be upon me (Ps. 90:17).

Only those with clean hands and a pure heart may enjoy Your presence (Ps. 24:3–4). Thank You for giving me Your Holy Spirit so that I may have the power to be holy just as You are holy (Lev. 11:45).

The one thing I desire is that I may dwell in Your house all the days of my life, to behold Your beauty, and to seek You in Your temple (Ps. 27:4). "Better is one day in your courts than a thousand elsewhere" (Ps. 84:10 NIV). As I see You in all Your beauty and splendor, I fall in love with You all over again.

So I pledge my allegiance to You my King and join the four living creatures surrounding Your throne who cry "Holy, holy, holy, / Lord God Almighty, / Who was and is and is to come!" (Rev. 4:8 NKJV).

See also:

1-2. Meditating on His Omnipotence and Omnipresence
1-3. Cherishing God's Love
1-4. Praising God for His Creation
2-3. Thanking God for the Cross and the Blood
3-1. Guarding Purity
3-2. Growing in Holiness
4. Sin

6

YEARNING FOR MORE OF JESUS

My soul yearns, even faints,
  for the courts of the LORD;
my heart and my flesh cry out
  for the living God.
(Ps. 84:2 NIV)

Dearest Jesus, I bring before You what is both a request and a gift. A request, because it benefits *me*. A gift, because it pleases *You*.

My heart's desire is for more of You. I readily confess that my ceaseless wanderings have proven that, apart from Your presence, I am spiritually bankrupt. Only in You have I found eternal life and truth (John 14:6). Only in You have I found the way to the Father's heart (John 14:6), and apart from You I have no good thing (Ps. 16:2).

You were the one whom the psalmist longed for:

Whom have I in heaven but you?
  And earth has nothing I desire besides you.
My flesh and my heart may fail,
  but God is the strength of my heart
  and my portion forever.
(Ps. 73:25–26 NIV)

Jesus, I desire only You because you are the strength of my heart and everything I will ever need—forever. My soul cries out for more of You because only in You do I find true purpose and meaning. You alone fit perfectly the God-shaped hole I so often try to fill with worldly and selfish pursuits.

So I echo John the Baptist's words: May You increase and I decrease (John 3:30). May You grow in me as I become less. And as I become less, live *Your* life through me. Only in that kind of life am I truly pleasing in Your sight.

"My soul longs, yes, even faints / For the courts of the LORD; / My heart and my flesh cry out for the living God" (Ps. 84:2 NKJV). Jesus, I thirst for the living water that comes only by drinking from the wells of salvation (Isa. 12:3).

I need more of You—more of Your power, more of Your glory, more of Your character, more of Your works. Lord Jesus, I need more of *You* in my life. I want to know You in the power of Your resurrection and the fellowship of Your sufferings, being conformed to Your death and so that somehow I may attain the resurrection of the dead (Phil 3:10). To know You is to love You, to live for You, and to die to my self.

Most of all, I want more of You simply because I love You.

See also:

1-7. Adoring Christ, the Great "I AM"
1-8. Worshiping in Spirit and Truth
2-1. Thanking God for Sending Jesus
2-10. Thanking God for Choosing Me
3-10. Finding Contentment
4-13. Dying to Selfishness

7

ADORING CHRIST, THE GREAT "I AM"

Jesus said to them, "Most assuredly, I say to you, before Abraham was, I AM." (John 8:58 NKJV)

Jesus, long ago when Moses encountered the burning bush on the side of Mt. Sinai, he was told "I AM WHO I AM" was sending him to save the children of Israel (Ex. 3:13–14). Little did he know that he was speaking to You. You were as present then as You were in the Gospels and as You are now (Heb. 13:8). You are not the great "I was" or the great "I wish"; You are the great "I AM." You reign in the ever present.

You are the bread of life (John 6:35). You promise that when I come to You I will never hunger and if I believe in You I will never thirst again because You completely satisfy my desires (John 4:13–14). No person, experience, or book nourishes me so completely as You do. You are my sole source of strength, and all other pursuits fail in utter pointlessness in comparison to You.

You are the light of the world (John 8:12). Jesus, You are pure, untainted and holy (1 John 1:5). Your light gives sight to my spiritual blindness and reveals to me the way of salvation. Apart from Your light, I wander aimlessly in darkness, but wherever Your light shines, the darkness flees, giving me clarity and direction.

You are the door for the sheep (John 10:9). In You I find protection and abundant supply. You are the only means of access into the safety, security, and salvation of the Father.

You are the good shepherd, and You take good care of Your sheep

(John 10:11). You aren't the *bad* shepherd, You are the *good* shepherd. When I wander away, You don't beat me, but You gently nudge me back onto Your paths. I may not always understand where You are leading, but I follow You because I know You are trustworthy. Even when I walk through the valley of the shadow of death, I fear no evil because You are my Protector (Ps. 23:4).

You are the resurrection and the life (John 11:25–26). Regardless of how discouraged I feel or how feeble my need appears, I am never without hope because You breathe life into lifeless situations. You are the Life-Giver, and Your power is stronger than even death and the grave (1 Cor. 15:55).

You are the way, the truth, and the life (John 14:6). I worship You and commit my life to You because You are the *only* way to eternal life. You are God's truth and God's life living in me.

You are the true vine (John 15:1). Any redeeming quality within me is a result of Your redeeming work (John 15:5–8). Without You, I can do nothing because I am solely dependent upon You (John 15:5). In love, You prune those parts of me that are unfruitful so that I can bear more fruit (John 15:2) and become more like You.

You are "I AM" because You are God—God's only son—clothed in human flesh (John 3:16). You're my Healer (Matt. 15:30), Redeemer (Gal. 4:4–5), Messiah (John 4:25–26), Savior (John 4:42), and Lord (1 Cor. 12:3). You are everything I want and everything I need. I praise You for being the great I AM!

See also:

1-6. Yearning for More of Jesus
2-1. Thanking God for Sending Jesus
2-8. Thanking God for Supplying my Needs
3-10. Finding Contentment
10-1. Supernatural Healing

8

WORSHIPING IN SPIRIT AND TRUTH

But the hour is coming, and now is, when the true worshipers will worship the Father in spirit and truth; for the Father is seeking such to worship Him. God is Spirit, and those who worship Him must worship in spirit and truth. (John 4:23–24 NKJV)

Father God, so often people confine their worship of You to specific times and places. But because You're not limited to a song I sing, a verse I read in the Bible, or a church service I attend, I refuse to live as if You are. Rather than entering Your presence a few times a week, I choose to take Your presence with me wherever I go. My heart longs to *live* in worship of You—to be a worshiper in spirit and truth.

I resolve to move past the lip service that so often permeates my life. "Let the words of my mouth and the meditation of my heart / Be acceptable in Your sight, / O LORD, my strength and my redeemer" (Ps. 19:14 NKJV). When I sleep and when I wake, may my first thought be You. When I drive on the road or labor in the workplace, may my thoughts gravitate to You because pleasing You is the only thing that matters.

Your Word exhorts me to offer my body as a living sacrifice, holy and pleasing to You—that this is my spiritual act of worship (Rom. 12:1). My visible expressions of devotion are not contingent upon those around me. What matters most is what You think because I am determined to please only one person: You.

Just as David danced through the streets of Jerusalem without concern for the opinions of those around Him, so I worship You with all that is within me (2 Sam. 6:14). My life is a stage performed for an audience of One. From attitude to ensuing action—in Spirit *and* in truth—let everything I think and do be pleasing to You.

Across the expanse of time and space, You call out to us, knowing that while worship pleases You, it transforms us as well. God, Your Word promises that You *seek out* those who worship You in spirit and truth (John 4:23–24). I want to be a person You seek. May Your creative, life-giving power infuse the words and actions I give to You.

See also:

1-5. Acclaiming God's Majesty and the Beauty of Holiness
2-6. Thanking God for Making Me the Righteousness of God in Christ
2-10. Thanking God for Choosing Me
3-2. Growing in Holiness
3-3. Bearing the Fruit of the Spirit
3-6. Learning Obedience
3-7. Developing Integrity
4-2. The Prayer of Recommitment
11. Bringing in the Kingdom of God

9

LOVING GOD'S WILL

In Him also we have obtained an inheritance, being predestined according to the purpose of Him who works all things according to the counsel of His will, that we who first trusted in Christ should be to the praise of His glory. (Eph. 1:11–12 NKJV)

Heavenly Father, I take comfort in knowing that the complexities of this world and the affairs of my life are not my responsibility to ultimately understand or control. Were I the master of this world's destiny, our very existence would be doomed.

But I glory in knowing that Your wisdom far surpasses mine. Your Word declares, "'For My thoughts are not your thoughts, / Nor are your ways My ways,' says the LORD. / 'For as the heavens are higher than the earth, / So are My ways higher than your ways, / And My thoughts than your thoughts'" (Isa. 55:8–9 NKJV).

You see the forest *and* the trees. Between orchestrating global politics and tending to my trivial concerns, You know intimately every person who lives or ever has lived, and You direct the affairs of every person according to Your divine plan.

You are the all-knowing, all-understanding God. The heavens and the earth are the creation of Your knowledge and power. By Your omniscience You determine the ultimate end of the just and the unjust. Your wisdom is not based upon the wisdom of this world, but according to wisdom from above. There is no wisdom, no insight, no plan that can succeed apart from You (Prov. 21:30 NIV).

Oh, the depth of the riches of the wisdom and knowledge of

God! How unsearchable Your judgments, and Your paths beyond tracing out! (Rom. 11:33 NIV). You have infinite wisdom.

Through Your Son Jesus, You created the heavens and the earth (John 1:1-3) and You sustain all things (Heb. 1:3).

Above all, Your crowning achievement of creation . . . was me. You knit me in my mother's womb (Ps. 139:13 NIV) creating me in Your image (Gen. 1:26–27), and You breathed into me Your breath of life (Gen. 2:7). You loved me so much You gave Your Son to die on a cross for my sins so that I can enjoy eternity with You (1 Peter 2:24).

You have infinite wisdom and ultimate power, but I love Your will because I know *You love me.* You're trustworthy. Whether I recognize it or not, You always act in my best interests. I love Your will because I know You always respond in love. You're on my side, and if You are for me, who can be against me (Rom. 8:31)?

When I don't understand, I will trust You. Even when circumstances seem harsh, I know You are working Your will out in my life because all things work together for good to those who love You and who are the called according to Your purpose (Rom. 8:28).

Therefore I can say with confidence: "Lord, may Your kingdom come and Your will be done in my life as it is in heaven" (Matt. 6:10).

"Now to the King eternal, immortal, invisible, to God who alone is wise, be honor and glory forever and ever. Amen" (1 Tim. 1:17 NKJV).

See also:

1-2. Meditating on His Omnipotence and Omnipresence
1-5. Acclaiming God's Majesty and the Beauty of Holiness
3-6. Learning Obedience
3-8. Joining God in His Will
4-15. Finding Freedom from Rebellion

10

REJOICING IN THE FACE OF DISCOURAGEMENT

Rejoice in the Lord always. Again I will say, rejoice!
(Phil. 4:4 NKJV)

Today I choose to look past my circumstances to the One who reigns over them. Jesus, despite the myriad emotions I may feel, I offer up to You a sacrifice of praise (Heb. 13:15). When my life is devoid of problems, the praise I give to You comes at an affordable price. However, when circumstances do not go according to *my* plans, that is when I dig deep to rejoice in You. I *will not* sacrifice to the Lord my God offerings of praise that cost me nothing (2 Sam. 24:24).

So I rejoice. I rejoice in the God of my salvation:

Though the fig tree may not blossom,
Nor fruit be on the vines;
Though the labor of the olive may fail,
And the fields yield no food;
Though the flock may be cut off from the fold,
And there be no herd in the stalls—
Yet I will rejoice in the LORD,
I will joy in the God of my salvation.
The LORD God is my strength;
He will make my feet like deer's feet,
And He will make me walk on my high hills.
(Hab. 3:17–19 NKJV)

Lord God, You are the One who gives me the feet of a deer. You are the One who makes me to walk on the high hills so I can scale any mountain.

Jesus, as You were crucified and buried, hope seemed lost, but within three days You were alive again with resurrection power. In the same way, I know the last chapter of my life has yet to be written.

As Paul and Silas sat shackled in the Philippian jail lifting up their voices in praise to Your name, the great and mighty power of Your hand set them free (Acts 16:25–26). Your praises shake the foundations of prisons, they break loose the ties that bind, and they set the captives free.

I will praise You in the face of my own inadequacies because in my weakness You are made strong (2 Cor. 12:10). You use difficult circumstances to plow up the fallow ground in my life. In fact, You do Your best creative work with chaos (Gen. 1:2).

At Your side is the only safe place. The circumstances I face may lie beyond my understanding, yet with confidence I can declare that *I trust You*. I desire to be by Your side regardless of the rising waves around me because I know at any moment You can speak to my storms and say, "Peace, be still!" (Mark 4:39) and the storms will be calmed.

So I rejoice! You are at work beyond what I can see. I, like Paul, am confident of this very thing: "that He who has begun a good work in me will complete it until the day of Jesus Christ" (Phil 1:6 NKJV).

See also:

1-1. Magnifying the Lord
2-8. Thanking God for Supplying my Needs
3-5. Producing Endurance
5-3. Hope for Despair
6-4. Financial Difficulties
10. Sickness and Disease

2

THANKING GOD FOR WHAT HE HAS DONE

One day, walking through a small village on his way to Jerusalem, Jesus heard a group of men yelling at Him over the tumult of the crowd. "Jesus!" "Master!" "Have mercy on us!"

Moved with compassion, Jesus looked over at the ten men afflicted with leprosy and said, "Go, show yourselves to the priests."

The lepers departed, and after being thoroughly examined by the priests—who also served as makeshift doctors—they were given a clean bill of health. Nine of the men ran off, most likely to their families, undoubtedly overjoyed with being delivered from a skin condition that had rendered them the outcasts of society. Being healed from leprosy was like to being given new life.

But only one man, a Samaritan, returned to Jesus. He fell down on his face at Jesus' feet and thanked Him.

Looking down at the man, Jesus asked, "Were there not ten cleansed? But where are the nine? Were there not any found who returned to give glory to God except this foreigner?" And He said to him, "Arise, go your way. Your faith has made you well" (Luke 17:11–19 NKJV).

Why was it so important to Jesus that all ten men return to thank Him?

As far back as the time of Moses, we can see that an attitude of thankfulness is important to God. One of the offerings the Israelites were commanded to bring before God was a thank offering. People presented a thank offering to God whenever they received an unsolicited blessing. It may have been an unexpected pregnancy or an exceptionally good harvest. Regardless, a thank offering represented an acknowledgment of gratitude for a gift undeserved. Through the time of Jesus, people brought thank offerings to God.

Later, on the night He was betrayed, Jesus and His disciples shared what we now call the Lord's Supper. One of the more traditional terms for this event is the word *Eucharist*. In the Greek language, the word *eucharista* means "thanksgiving." We share the Lord's Supper remembering the greatest gift of all: Jesus.

Thanksgiving is different than worship and praise. Worship focuses on *who* God is—His inherent attributes and character (see Chap. 1). Thanksgiving, on the other hand, focuses on *what* He has done. We praise God for His *ability* to meet our needs. We thank Him for *meeting* our needs. Both are intrinsic to effective prayer.

The Psalmist wrote, "Enter into His gates with thanksgiving, / And into His courts with praise. / Be thankful to Him, *and* bless His name" (Ps. 100:4 NKJV). Together, they comprise our means of entering into the presence of God.

Like those ten lepers, we have been given new life from Jesus Christ. We, as much as they, have much to be thankful for.

1

THANKING GOD FOR SENDING JESUS

Let this mind be in you which was also in Christ Jesus, who, being in the form of God, did not consider it robbery to be equal with God, but made Himself of no reputation, taking the form of a servant, and coming in the likeness of men. And being found in appearance as a man, He humbled Himself and became obedient to the point of death, even the death of the cross. (Phil. 2:5–8 NKJV)

Lord Jesus, I will never fully comprehend why You chose to leave the comfort and security of heaven to come to earth. Why would You set aside Your divinity, take the form of a bondservant, clothe Yourself in human flesh, and humble Yourself to the point of being nailed to a cross (Phil 2:6–8)? It could only be the result of a love I will never understand. But I am eternally grateful.

You willingly obeyed the will of Your Father and chose to be born of the Virgin Mary in order to redeem me—to buy me back—from the law of sin and death. Though You were rich, yet for my sake You became poor, so that through Your poverty I might become rich (2 Cor. 8:9). You weren't born of wealthy parents, You had no beauty that we should desire You; You were despised and rejected by men, a man of sorrows and acquainted with grief (Isa. 53:2–3).

You didn't wait for us to recognize You, esteem You, or acknowledge You for who You were. But You welcomed me into the family of God as Your adopted sibling (Gal. 4:4–5), and through faith in You I am a child of God as well (Gal. 3:26).

I can now approach the throne of grace knowing You identify exactly with my need. When I face temptation, I know You will make available to me Your mercy and grace in abundant supply because You were tempted in all points as I am, yet You were without sin (Heb. 4:15–16). When I encounter stressful situations, I know Your grace is sufficient for me (2 Cor. 12:8–9) because You endured the stress of going to the cross. When I encounter rejection (John 1:11), hardships (2 Cor. 1:5), and extreme need (Phil. 4:19), I know in You I have a High Priest who sympathizes with my weaknesses.

Thank You for sparing no expense—even at the cost of Your own life—in order to understand me, make salvation available to me, and show me the way to the Father. My only response is to live for You.

See also:

1-6. Yearning for More of Jesus
1-7. Adoring Christ, the Great "I AM"
2-3. Thanking God for the Cross and the Blood
2-6. Thanking God for Making Me the Righteousness of God in Christ
4-1. The Prayer of Salvation (Sinner's Prayer)
11-2. Sharing the Gospel
11-10. The Second Coming of Christ

2

THANKING GOD FOR HIS WORD

> All Scripture is given by inspiration of God, and is profitable for doctrine, for reproof, for correction, for instruction in righteousness, that the man of God may be complete, thoroughly equipped for every good work. (2 Tim. 3:16–17 NKJV)

Lord God, my heart echoes the reflections of the psalmist, "I *love* Your Word" (Ps. 119:97). Like a delectable morsel of food, I savor every bit. "How sweet are Your words to my taste, / Sweeter than honey to my mouth!" (Ps. 119:103 NKJV). The longer I go without it, the weaker my spirit becomes and the harder my heart grows. But feasting upon Your Word, I grow stronger and more sensitive to Your Spirit.

Your Word is the standard of all truth. "The entirety of Your word is truth, / And every one of Your righteous judgments endures forever" (Ps. 119:160 NKJV). All truth must agree with Your Word, or it isn't truth.

Your Word stands immovable and eternal. "The grass withers, the flower fades, / But the word of our God stands forever" (Isa. 40:8 NKJV). There is no other book like the Bible. In a society where beliefs and morality change like the seasons, You give me a solid foundation to stand on that weathers any storm.

Your Word shows me the way of salvation. Without it, I wouldn't know the keys to eternal life and I wouldn't know You (2 Tim. 3:15). Jesus, thank You for revealing Yourself to me through Scripture.

Your Word strengthens me in my fight against sin. "Your word I have hidden in my heart, / That I might not sin against You" (Ps. 119:11 NKJV).

Your Word gives me direction. "Your word is a lamp to my feet / And a light to my path" (Ps. 119:105 NKJV).

Your Word infuses me with hope. "For whatever things were written before were written for our learning, that we through the patience and comfort of the Scriptures might have hope" (Rom. 15:4 NKJV). When I am discouraged I can open up Your Word and learn more of Your love for me.

Your Word brings prosperity. As I meditate on Your Word and obey all that is written in it, my way becomes prosperous and I have good success (Josh. 1:8).

The power of Your Word defeats the enemy. I thank You for placing into my hands the sword of the Spirit, which is the Word of God (Eph. 6:17), enabling me to conquer the forces of Satan and hell.

Lord God, Your Word is living and powerful, sharper than any two-edged sword, piercing even to the division of soul and spirit, and of joints and marrow, and is a discerner of the thoughts and intents of the heart (Heb. 4:12). Your Word opens up my heart to the inner workings of Your Holy Spirit.

Thank You for entrusting to me Your life-giving Word and for loving me enough to reveal Your character and Your ways.

See also:

1-6. Yearning for More of Jesus
1-9. Loving God's Will
3-8. Joining God in His Will
3-9. Building Faith and Trust
4-1. The Prayer of Salvation (Sinner's Prayer)
4-2. The Prayer of Recommitment
4-14. Liberty from Lying and Deceit
5-3. Hope for Despair
6-4. Financial Difficulties
6-8. Direction for the Future

3

THANKING GOD FOR THE CROSS AND THE BLOOD

For it pleased the Father that in [Christ] all the fullness should dwell, and by Him to reconcile all things to Himself, by Him, whether things on earth or things in heaven, having made peace through the blood of His cross. (Col. 1:19–20 NKJV)

Lord Jesus, what is the measure of Your love for me? Tainted by sin, I was unclean and unfit to spend eternity with You. Undeserving of Your mercy and grace, all I had to look forward to was a death sentence of eternity in hell. There was no way I could save myself.

But Jesus, You demonstrated the full extent of Your love by offering Yourself as the pure and spotless sacrifice (John 13:1). You willingly endured the cross, despising its shame, just for me (Heb. 12:2). In Your death, I died with You. Thank You that I am now dead to sin, but alive to righteousness (Rom. 6:8–13). By identifying with me on the cross, I now have the power to live for You (Gal. 2:20).

With Your blood You purchased me, paying the penalty for my sin (Acts 20:28). Though my sins were like scarlet, now they are white as snow (Isa. 1:18). Thank You that as far as the east is from the west is how far You have removed my transgressions away from me (Ps. 103:12). By Your blood I am justified and saved from wrath (Rom. 5:9). You were wounded for my transgressions, You were bruised for my iniquities; the chastisement for my peace was upon You, and by Your stripes I am healed (Isa. 53:5).

In Your atoning blood I find healing. My relationship is restored to the Father (Col. 1:19–20). Body, mind, and spirit, I am whole and complete (Col. 2:10). Thank You that I can now enter boldly into the Holy of Holies by the blood of Jesus (Heb. 10:19).

On that dark night in the garden of Gethsemane, You laid aside Your will in order to save me (Luke 22:42). You could have bypassed the Cross. You could have explained Your way out of the mock trial. You could have averted the beatings. You could have circumvented the crown of thorns and the stripes on Your back. You could have avoided taking a spear in Your side. You could have stepped off that cross and destroyed the human race. But You didn't. Hanging on that cross, You looked down on humanity—the very people who were persecuting You—and You asked for Your Father to forgive them. You could have displayed no greater love than to suffer and die on *my* behalf (John 15:13). Hanging on that cross, I know that You thought of me, You suffered for me, and You died for me.

Thank You, Jesus, for the Cross and the blood. You have delivered me from the power of darkness and conveyed *me* into the kingdom of the Son (Col. 1:13–14).

See also:

1-3. Cherishing God's Love
2-1. Thanking God for Sending Jesus
2-6. Thanking God for Making Me the Righteousness of God in Christ
4. Sin
6-3. Conflict Between Husband and Wife
8-1. Healing Strained Relationships with Parents
8-2. Mending Broken Friendships
10. Sickness and Disease

4

THANKING GOD FOR HIS GRACE AND MERCY

Let us therefore come boldly to the throne of grace, that we may obtain mercy and find grace to help in time of need. (Heb. 4:16 NKJV)

God of mercy and grace, I come before You in humble gratitude. I am fully aware of my gravitation toward evil. My sinful nature deserves no less than eternal damnation.

Thank You for not giving me what I deserve. The wages of sin is death—eternity in hell—but You have shown the abundance of Your mercy by giving me the free gift of eternal life in Christ Jesus (Rom. 6:23). I don't have to worry that You are hovering over me, waiting to punish every stray thought or false deed, for Your Word tells me, "The LORD is gracious and full of compassion, / Slow to anger and great in mercy. / The LORD is good to all, / And His tender mercies are over all His works" (Ps. 145:8–9 NKJV).

Over and over, I test the limits of Your love, and repeatedly You show to me that Your mercy comes in bountiful supply. Through Your mercies I am not consumed, because Your compassions *never* fail. They are new every morning. Each day presents new insights into Your lovingkindness. My heart can't help but cry out, "Great is Your faithfulness" (Lam. 3:22–23). "Oh, give thanks to the LORD, for He is good! / For His mercy endures forever" (1 Chron. 16:34 NKJV).

You could have stopped showing me mercy at the point of

salvation. But You didn't. Although You owe me nothing, You have also granted to me the abundance of Your grace.

Thank You for giving me what I don't deserve. I am truly the recipient of Your unmerited favor. I find security in knowing there is nothing I can do to earn any more of Your love (Rom. 11:5–6). You offer it freely to all people—righteous and unrighteous alike (1 Peter 3:18).

By Your grace You have endowed me with the gifts of Your Holy Spirit and the power to do Your works in Jesus' name. Healing, prophecy, discernment, words of knowledge—all are grace gifts revealing the work of Your Spirit (1 Cor. 12:7–10). Any good deed I commit, any encouraging word I give, anything redeemable in my life is the result of Your grace working through me (1 Cor. 15:10).

You show me even little works of grace that reaffirm Your love. You give me wisdom when I am confused. You comfort me when I am discouraged. Even in my moments of weakness I take heart because You have promised me "My grace is sufficient for you, for My strength is made perfect in weakness" (2 Cor. 12:9 NKJV). Thank You for giving me the grace I need to overcome any obstacle.

See also:

1-3. Cherishing God's Love
1-4. Praising God for His Creation
2-1. Thanking God for Sending Jesus
2-3. Thanking God for the Cross and the Blood
2-10. Thanking God for Choosing Me
3-4. Moving in the Gifts of the Spirit
4. Sin
10. Sickness and Disease

5

THANKING GOD FOR THE RESURRECTION OF CHRIST

But if the Spirit of Him who raised Jesus from the dead dwells in you, He who raised Christ from the dead will also give life to your mortal bodies through His Spirit who dwells in you. (Rom. 8:11 NKJV)

Hallelujah! Jesus, You're alive!

Thank You, heavenly Father, for giving Your Son, Jesus, to die on the cross for me. But had His body remained in the tomb, my faith would be rendered worthless and I, above all people, would be most pitied (1 Cor. 15:17–19). I need hope that transcends the grave.

Jesus, when You emerged from the tomb on the third day You opened up for me the portals of heaven that lead to eternal life. Thank You that I can know with confidence that eternal life belongs to me as I confess You as Lord and believe God raised You from the dead (1 John 5:13; Rom. 10:9). The eternal life You have given me cannot be taken away (John 10:28).

I revel in enjoying the benefits of eternal life right now. I am never beyond hope because my trust resides in the *living* hope (1 Peter 1:3). Through the Holy Spirit, that same resurrection power is working within me. Sickness and suffering are no match for Your life-giving power. Now, at the name of Jesus, every knee must bow in heaven and on earth and under the earth, and every tongue confess that Jesus Christ is Lord, to the glory of God the

Father (Phil. 2:10–11). Because of Your resurrection, Satan has *no* power over me!

Death has died (Rom. 6:9). You proved once and forever that there is no force greater than You. Lord Jesus, You are the resurrection and the life (John 11:25). No longer do I fear the grave because death is swallowed up in victory. "O Death, where is your sting? O Hades, where is your victory?" The sting of death is sin, and the strength of sin is the law. But thanks be to God, who gives me the victory through our Lord Jesus Christ (1 Cor. 15:54–57)! Lord Jesus, You hold in Your hands the keys to death and Hades (Rev. 1:18). And someday soon You will cast Satan and his minions into the lake of fire and throw away the keys forever (Rev. 20:14–15).

Jesus, You won! Satan is under my feet, and the victory is mine through my faith in You (Rom. 16:20). You came to earth to destroy the works of the devil, and You succeeded (1 John 3:8). Thank You for including me in the benefits of Your victory.

See also:

1-2. Meditating on His Omnipotence and Omnipresence
1-7. Adoring Christ, the Great "I AM"
2-3. Thanking God for the Cross and the Blood
2-7. Thanking God for Sending His Spirit
4. Sin
10. Sickness and Disease
11-10. The Second Coming of Christ

6

THANKING GOD FOR MAKING ME THE RIGHTEOUSNESS OF GOD IN CHRIST

For whom He foreknew, He also predestined to be conformed to the image of His Son, that He might be the firstborn among many brethren. (Rom. 8:29 NKJV)

Heavenly Father, I come before You in the name of Jesus with a grateful heart. You have shared the riches of heaven and blessed me with every spiritual blessing in Christ. Sin had estranged me from You, but You have taken me in and adopted me as Your very own child (Eph. 1:3–6). Now I am seated in the heavenly places (Eph. 2:6) and reign with You as an heir of God and a coheir with Jesus Christ (2 Tim. 2:12; Rom. 8:17). The depths of Your mercy and grace are far greater than I could ever comprehend.

Not only have You seated me with You in the high places, but You have also given me the identity of Your Son. Your Word tells me, "For He made Him who knew no sin to be sin for us, that we might become the righteousness of God in Him" (2 Cor. 5:21 NKJV). Thank You for making *Your* righteousness *my* righteousness. I am now the righteousness of God in Christ! When You look at me, You see me through the blood of Jesus. You accept me as if I were Jesus. You love me as You love Jesus. And slowly You are transforming me into His image so when I see You face to face, I will truly be like Him (2 Cor 3:18).

Because of Jesus I am sanctified (set apart and made holy), justified (declared completely forgiven—1 Cor. 6:11), accepted by the Father (Eph. 1:6), and complete (Col. 2:9–10). You have even allowed me to participate in Your divine nature (2 Peter 1:4).

No longer do I take my identity from what I do, what I've done, or what has been done to me; I now find my identity in You. I am *Your* workmanship, a creation of the Master Builder, created in Christ Jesus for good works (Eph. 2:10). Because I am in Christ, I am a different person, the old things have passed away; behold, all things have become new (2 Cor. 5:17). My life is now hidden with Christ in God (Col. 3:3). You have shown me the exceeding riches of Your grace and Your kindness toward me in Christ Jesus.

Father God, thank You for calling me Your own, loving me like Your only Son, and giving me Your identity.

See also:

1-3. Cherishing God's Love
1-7. Adoring Christ, the Great "I AM"
2-1. Thanking God for Sending Jesus
2-3. Thanking God for the Cross and the Blood
2-5. Thanking God for the Resurrection of Christ
2-10. Thanking God for Choosing Me
3-1. Guarding Purity
6-7. Physical or Emotional Abuse
8-4. Feeling Abandoned and Rejected

7

THANKING GOD FOR SENDING HIS SPIRIT

But if the Spirit of Him who raised Jesus from the dead dwells in you, He who raised Christ from the dead will also give life to your mortal bodies through His Spirit who dwells in you. (Rom. 8:11 NKJV)

Lord Jesus, while You ministered here on earth, You willingly laid aside Your divine rights (Phil. 2:5–8) relying upon the Holy Spirit to accomplish Your miraculous works (Luke 4:14). For Your crowning achievement, on the third day the Spirit raised You up from the grave with resurrection power. I, in chorus with all creation, rejoice at Your victory over death and the grave! And equally amazing, at Pentecost You bequeathed to Your followers that same power (Rom. 8:11), filling them with Your Holy Spirit (Acts 2:4). Now I live *Your* life empowered by the same Holy Spirit.

Thank You for infusing into me a part of Yourself. Had You not gone to be with the Father (John 16:7), I would have never been able to enjoy basking in the river of Your Spirit (Ezek. 47:1–12). Every day Your Spirit makes me thirsty for more of You so that I cannot help but cry out "Abba, Father!" (Gal. 4:6). Knowing my experience with Your Spirit is a deposit, a down payment, of better things to come makes me grow in even greater anticipation of spending eternity with You (Eph. 1:13–14). I long to be with You, to please You, and to be more like You.

Gracious God, how would I grasp the magnitude of my sin unless Your Holy Spirit convicted me (John 16:8)? How would I know the sacrificial love of Your Son and the gift of eternal life, unless Your Spirit revealed Jesus to me (John 14:26)? How could I walk in purity without Your Spirit giving me strength for holiness (Rom. 8:13)? How could I know Your comfort without the Comforter who comes alongside me (Acts 9:31)?

When I am troubled and don't know how to pray, Your Spirit intercedes on my behalf (Rom. 8:26). When I am confused Your Spirit guides me into Your truth (John 16:13). When I feel powerless, Your Spirit gives me the power to be Your witness in sharing the good news of salvation in Jesus (Acts 1:8). Through Your Spirit, I find liberty and freedom from sin and legalism (2 Cor. 3:17).

I know You aren't content to leave me as I am, but You promise to continue shaping me and molding me into Your image (Phil. 1:6). May the fruit of Your Spirit's work *in* me produce Your character (Gal. 5:22–23), and may Your Spirit's ministering *through* me manifest in spiritual gifts so that I can live and minister like Jesus (1 Cor. 12:4–11).

The work of Your Spirit in me is never ending. I have tasted and I can say that the Lord is good (Ps. 34:8)!

See also:

1-2. Meditating on His Omnipotence and Omnipresence
1-5. Acclaiming God's Majesty and the Beauty of Holiness
1-8. Worshiping in Spirit and Truth
2-5. Thanking God for the Resurrection of Christ
3-2. Growing in Holiness
3-3. Bearing the Fruit of the Spirit
3-4. Moving in the Gifts of the Spirit
4. Sin
10. Sickness and Disease
11-1. Revival in the Church
11-2. Sharing the Gospel
11-7. Outpouring of Signs and Wonders

8

THANKING GOD FOR SUPPLYING MY NEEDS

Now may He who supplies seed to the sower, and bread for food, supply and multiply the seed you have sown and increase the fruits of your righteousness, while you are enriched in everything for all liberality, which causes thanksgiving through us to God. (2 Cor. 9:10–11 NKJV)

Great and mighty God, Your Word assures me that You will supply all my needs according to Your riches by Christ Jesus (Phil. 4:19). I thank You that You *have* supplied my needs.

My greatest need was my debt of sin. I was over my head in debt without any means of repaying You, and You generously paid it (Luke 7:41–42). Thank You for supplying my greatest need with the ultimate sacrificial lamb—Your Son, Jesus (Heb. 10:10). You have spared no expense to save me.

You supplied manna in the wilderness for the children of Israel (Ex. 16:14–17), and You continue to supply me with spiritual manna whenever I face my own wilderness. You have generously shared with me from the abundance of Your limitless resources: food that gives me strength, clothes that keep me warm, and shelter that protects me from harm. I have no reason to fear the future because I have witnessed Your faithfulness in the past and I know You hold me in the palm of Your hand.

With a grateful heart I thank You for . . .

(Now take a moment to bless God by thanking Him for as many things as you possibly can, including: spiritual blessings and insights, enriching relationships, unexpected answers to prayer, etc.)

Every good gift and every perfect gift is from above and comes down from the Father of lights, with whom there is no variation or shadow of turning (James 1:17). I recognize that You have supplied all my needs.

This day I join with the angels, elders, and the four living creatures surrounding the throne, worshiping You and saying,

> Amen! Blessing and glory and wisdom,
> Thanksgiving and honor and power and might,
> Be to our God forever and ever.
> Amen. (Rev. 7:12 NKJV)

See also:

1-7. Adoring Christ, the Great "I AM"
1-10. Rejoicing in the Face of Discouragement
2-3. Thanking God for the Cross and the Blood
3-10. Finding Contentment
4-6. Triumphing over Greed, Indulgence, and Materialism
4-9. Giving God Control of Selfish Ambition
6-4. Financial Difficulties
9-6. Favor
10-9. When God Doesn't Heal
11-3. Compassion for the Poor and Needy

9

THANKING GOD FOR HIS PROTECTION

Because you have made the LORD, who is my refuge,
Even the Most High, your habitation,
No evil shall befall you,
Nor shall any plague come near your dwelling;
For He shall give His angels charge over you,
To keep you in all your ways . . .
Because he has set his love upon Me,
therefore I will deliver him;
I will set him on high, because he has known My name.
He shall call upon Me, and I will answer him;
I will be with him in trouble;
I will deliver him and honor him.
With long life I will satisfy him,
And show him My salvation.
(Ps. 91:9–11, 14–16 NKJV)

Almighty God, You are my refuge and my dwelling place. I have no reason to fear that evil will come upon me nor that any sickness or disease will come near me. Thank You for dispatching Your angels to guard me, uphold me, and to keep me from falling. I know that because You are with me I can venture where angels fear to tread.

When I am in distress, I know that I can call upon You and You will answer me. You walk with me in the middle of my trouble, preserving me from harm, and surrounding me with songs of assurance and deliverance. Lord God, You are my hiding place (Ps. 32:7). I have found You to be a strong tower where I can run and be safe (Prov. 18:10).

I rest knowing that nothing wicked can touch me except what comes through You (1 John 5:18). You have never abandoned me in the past, and I know You never will in the future because Your Word promises You will never leave me nor forsake me (Heb. 13:5). Never does evil or harm have permission to snatch me out of Your hand because You are greater than any danger (John 10:29).

You have given me the armor of God so that when the day of evil inevitably comes, I *will stand!* You have placed the sword of the Spirit and the shield of faith in my hands to defeat the powers of evil and quench Satan's fiery darts (Eph. 6:16). I am never alone. And when the enemy comes in like a flood, You lift up a standard against him (Isa. 59:19).

But most of all, I know I have nothing to fear because of Your great love for me. If You know the number of hairs on my head and You care for me more than the sparrow that falls to the ground (Matt. 10:29–31), why should I be afraid?

Thank You for covering me with Your love and Your protection.

See also:

1-1. Magnifying the Lord
1-2. Meditating on His Omnipotence and Omnipresence
2-8. Thanking God for Supplying My Needs
3-9. Building Faith and Trust
5-2. Peace for Worry
7-7. For the Protection of Your Children
9-5. Travel for Business
10-6. Protection from Sickness and Disease

10

THANKING GOD FOR CHOOSING ME

> But we are bound to give thanks to God always for you, brethren beloved by the Lord, because God from the beginning chose you for salvation through sanctification by the Spirit and belief in the truth, to which He called you by our gospel, for the obtaining of the glory of our Lord Jesus Christ. (2 Thess. 2:13–14 NKJV)

Gracious God, without Your promise of salvation, I would be condemned to an eternity in hell. Yet, even before the foundations of the world were established, You knew me and You chose me. Like a proud expectant parent, Your plans for my life far exceeded anything my mind could ever conceive (Jer. 29:11; Eph. 3:20–21). Out on my own, there was no way I would ever find You except for the gentle whisperings of Your Holy Spirit drawing me to You. When I ignored Your pleadings, You continued pursuing me because Your persistent love is stronger than my ability to outrun You. Like a helpless newborn, I did nothing to merit Your favor but You poured out Your love on me with generosity and without finding fault.

Your Word tells me how much I mean to You: "For you know the grace of our Lord Jesus Christ, that though He was rich, yet for your sakes He became poor, that you through His poverty might become rich" (2 Cor. 8:9). You were the prince who became a pauper so that this pauper could live as a prince with You in eternity. God, I am grateful to You for choosing me to receive eternal life and seating me with You in the high places (Eph. 2:6).

Because You have chosen me I don't have to be concerned whether I'll ever be good enough to be worthy of Your love. I know I'm not, but I also know that Your grace is sufficient for me (2 Cor. 12:9). Your love is more than enough. Because You have chosen me, my identity now resides in You.

Your Word reveals the extent of Your plans for me and my true identity:

> But you are a chosen generation, a royal priesthood, a holy nation, His own special people, that you may proclaim the praises of Him who called you out of darkness into His marvelous light. (1 Peter 2:9 NKJV)

In my chosenness You have given me a mandate to be holy and blameless (Eph. 1:4–6), to bear fruit that will last (John 15:16), and to partner with You in establishing Your kingdom (2 Cor. 6:1).

You knew me. You formed me. You accepted me. You gave me Your identity. You gave me purpose by including me in Your work. I know I am special because You are special. *Lord, thank You for choosing me.*

See also:

1-3. Cherishing God's Love
1-6. Yearning for More of Jesus
1-7. Adoring Christ, the Great "I AM"
2-1. Thanking God for Sending Jesus
2-3. Thanking God for the Cross and the Blood
2-4. Thanking God for His Grace and Mercy
11-8. World Harvest

3

BECOMING MORE LIKE JESUS

Prayer that moves mountains is grounded in bringing the issues to God that are on *His* heart. Jesus said in John 15:7, "If you abide in Me, and My words abide in you, you will ask what you desire, and it shall be done for you" NKJV. Abiding in God means to commune with Him and nurture a continuing relationship with Him. It implies discerning first what are the issues on His heart and then making those desires ours. By doing this, we join our prayers to God's power.

Watchman Nee, the well-known Christian leader from China once wrote,

> What then is the prayer ministry of the church? It is God telling the church what He wants to do and the church praying on earth what God wants to do. This prayer is not asking God to accomplish what we want Him to do, but asking God to accomplish what He Himself wants to do.[1]

God's primary desire is to make us more like Him, to mold us into the image of His Son. We begin this by giving to Him our will. In our time of prayer, we give God room to cleanse areas of our lives that need cleaning. He desires to work *in* us, and then *through* us.

The psalmist wrote, "Delight yourself also in the LORD, / And He shall give you the desires of your heart" (Ps. 37:4 NKJV). Delighting in the Lord means to enjoy Him and to do the things that please Him. If imitation is the sincerest form of flattery, then seeking to become like Jesus pleases the Father above all else. The Contemporary English Version succinctly paraphrases this same Scripture: "Do what the LORD wants, / and he will give you your heart's desire."

As we lay our will and our agenda before God, becoming more like Christ, God gives us our desires—because our desires have become conformed with His.

1

GUARDING PURITY

Who may ascend into the hill of the LORD?
Or who may stand in His holy place?
He who has clean hands and a pure heart,
Who has not lifted up his soul to an idol,
Nor sworn deceitfully.
He shall receive blessing from the LORD,
And righteousness from the God of his salvation.
This is Jacob, the generation of those who seek Him,
Who seek Your face.
Selah
Lift up your heads, O you gates!
And be lifted up, you everlasting doors!
And the King of glory shall come in. (Ps. 24:3–7 NKJV)

Jesus, You said only the pure in heart will see God (Matt. 5:8). Lord, I want to see You. I want to see Your face and I'm willing to do whatever it takes to behold You in all Your glory and majesty.

Shield me from the pollution and the indelible stain of sin that comes from the ways of this world. Guard my purity, beginning in my mind, and let it course through the rest of my body. Examine every stray imagination and errant motive until every thought is brought into captivity to the obedience of Christ (2 Cor. 10:5).

Lord, I need Your eyes to discern the deceptive allure of sin that hides Your face from me (Isa. 59:2). I need Your Spirit to guide my mind to those things which are true, noble, just, pure, lovely, of good report, virtuous, and praiseworthy (Phil 4:8). And most of all, I need Your strength to abstain from every form of evil (1 Thess. 5:22).

Your divine power has given me everything I need for life and godliness through my knowledge of You (2 Peter 1:3–4). My heart's desire is to keep my life pure by living according to Your Word (Ps. 119:9).

I realize I am a work in progress. May nothing stand in the way of my pursuit in knowing You, pleasing You, and seeing You in all Your glory.

See also:

1-5. Acclaiming God's Majesty and the Beauty of Holiness
1-8. Worshiping in Spirit and Truth
2-3. Thanking God for the Cross and the Blood
2-6. Thanking God for Making Me the Righteousness of God in Christ
2-7. Thanking God for Sending His Spirit
3-2. Growing in Holiness
3-7. Developing Integrity
4-4. Deliverance from Sexual Perversion
4-16. Fleeing Temptation

2

GROWING IN HOLINESS

He who has My commandments and keeps them, it is he who loves Me. And he who loves Me will be loved by My Father, and I will love him and manifest Myself to him. (John 14:21 NKJV)

Without holiness, Your Word tells me, no one will see the Lord (Heb. 12:14). Because I want to see You, I pursue Your holiness.

Holy God, thank You for conferring upon me Your righteousness and holiness (2 Cor. 5:21). Because of Your grace and mercy, You see me as holy despite my besetting struggle with sin. I sense You calling me to be what You already see in me. Like a butterfly emerging from a cocoon, may I become what I already am. And may the consummation of Your Spirit's work in me reveal the beauty of Your holiness (Ps. 96:6).

So often I flutter around asking You to show me Your will when I repeatedly ignore what I already know *is* Your will. Your will is that I be holy (Rom. 12:1–2).

Place within me a yearning for more of You and Your holy character, and create within me a dissatisfaction to remain where I am now. Examine my thoughts and intents, and sweep out all the impurities from the recesses and dark corners of my life. May my sin become as detestable to me as it is to You. I want to love what You love and hate what You hate. I want my actions to be congruent with my intentions. I want to be holy just as You are holy (1 Peter 1:15–16).

Steer me away from empty legalism that demands a righteous

lifestyle devoid of a relationship with You. Your holiness isn't something I disdain, Lord; it is beautiful. Your holiness reflects Your character just as the degree of my holiness does mine. I want nothing to stand in the way between You and me (Isa. 59:2).

Lord Jesus, You call me to deny myself, take up my cross daily, and follow You (Luke 9:23). I willingly choose to take up my cross and lay aside my own selfish desires so that I can say in all sincerity, just as the apostle Paul did:

> I have been crucified with Christ; it is no longer I who live, but Christ lives in me; and the life which I now live in the flesh I live by faith in the Son of God, who loved me and gave Himself for me. (Gal. 2:20 NKJV)

Apart from Your intervention, I cannot be the person You desire me to be. But by the power of Your Spirit, I can do all things through Christ who strengthens me (Phil. 4:13). I can be holy because nothing is impossible with Christ. Lord, sanctify me—set me apart—for Your work.

See also:

1-5. Acclaiming God's Majesty and the Beauty of Holiness
1-6. Yearning for More of Jesus
1-8. Worshiping in Spirit and Truth
2-6. Thanking God for Making Me the Righteousness of God in Christ
2-7. Thanking God for Sending His Spirit
3-1. Guarding Purity
3-3. Bearing the Fruit of the Spirit
4. Sin
11-1. Revival in the Church

3

BEARING THE FRUIT OF THE SPIRIT

But the fruit of the Spirit is love, joy, peace, longsuffering, kindness, goodness, faithfulness, gentleness, self-control. Against such there is no law. (Gal. 5:22–23 NKJV)

Heavenly Father, because I love You, I long to be more like You. May the fruit of our relationship yield Your divine character in me. I know that I can't generate it on my own—all too often my futile attempts result in a total crop failure. Any fruit is the product of Your Holy Spirit's work. So I open up my life to the transforming power of Your Spirit.

I realize the magnitude of Your character in my life is the measure of my spiritual maturity. My heart's desire is to respond to others and to You in a way that brings You pleasure and glory.

Work Your self-sacrificing *love* in my life. I know that I love others only to the extent that I love You. So fill me with Your love; show me the depths of Your love; love other people through me . . . because You are love (1 John 4:8).

When I face hardships and confusion, Your *joy* gives me strength (Neh. 8:10). Immerse me in Your joy so that my disposition and conduct are independent of ever-changing circumstances.

Let Your *peace*, which surpasses all understanding, guard my heart and mind through Christ Jesus (Phil. 4:7) so that in every situation I will have the assurance that You are in control. And may the peace You bring flow into my relationships (Heb. 12:14).

Your Word assures me that You aren't slow concerning Your

promised return, but You are *longsuffering*—patient—not willing that any should perish but that all should come to repentance (2 Peter 3:9). Give me Your eternal perspective so that I don't give up or force my way through Your will or other people's plans.

It's Your *kindness* that leads me to repentance (Rom. 2:4 NIV). So often I fail to respond to others befitting the kindness You consistently show me. May my actions draw others to the One who exemplifies kindness (Eph. 2:6–7).

Because You are good, I don't have to live in fear of You. Infuse me with Your *goodness* so I can respond to those around me with generosity, sincerity, and selfless motives (Eph. 5:9).

Even when I am faithless, You remain faithful because You cannot deny Yourself (2 Tim. 2:13). Please instill within me Your dependability and devotion so that, when everyone else is conceding defeat, I can exhibit the *faithfulness* You have shown me.

Through the ministry of Your Holy Spirit, You deal with me in all tenderness and compassion. Clothe me with Your *gentleness* so Your Spirit can use me as a vessel of Your love (Col. 3:12 NIV).

Place a guard over my thoughts, emotions, and actions so I won't give the enemy a foothold into my life (1 Peter 5:8). Give me Your *self-control* as I give my control over to You (2 Peter 1:5–7).

I want to crucify my flesh with its passions and desires. Show me how to live and walk in Your Spirit (Gal. 5:24–25).

See also:

1-8. Worshiping in Spirit and Truth
2-7. Thanking God for Sending His Spirit
3-2. Growing in Holiness
3-4. Moving in the Gifts of the Spirit
5-2. Peace for Worry
5-5. Control for Panic

4

MOVING IN THE GIFTS OF THE SPIRIT

> Follow the way of love and eagerly desire spiritual gifts. (1 Cor. 14:1 NIV)

Lord Jesus, during Your earthly ministry, You demonstrated kingdom living by touching people through the power of the Spirit: You gave sight to the blind, You raised the dead, You made the lame walk again (Luke 7:22). You healed and You preached the good news of the kingdom because You were moved with compassion for us (Matt. 14:14). As an agent of Your kingdom here on earth, I seek to continue where You left off.

I want to manifest Your character, but I also want to do Your works. I want the fruit of the Spirit (Gal. 5:22–23), but I want to move in the gifts of the Spirit (1 Cor. 12) as well. This isn't a selfish prayer because Your Word exhorts me to "desire spiritual gifts" (1 Cor. 14:1). Jesus, I stand on the faithful promise:

> Most assuredly, I say to you, he who believes in Me, the works that I do he will do also; and greater works than these he will do, because I go to My Father. (John 14:12 NKJV)

Lord Jesus, please use me as a vessel, a conduit of Your Holy Spirit that Your kingdom would reign through me here on earth. No longer will I be satisfied sitting on the sidelines watching You move in grace and with power. My heart yearns to join You in Your will and move with the flow of Your Spirit's work in this world. I'm asking for Your greater works and to operate in the gifts of Your Spirit, not for my own benefit but for Your glory.

Mighty God, increase the measure of my faith to believe You can use me beyond my past successes and failures. Instill within me a steadfast trust in You so I can minister in God-based confidence even when the results of my efforts appear as if nothing has changed. Grant me the humility to recognize that the degree of Your spiritual gifts in me are not a gauge of maturity but simply "grace gifts," which You distribute freely as You desire (1 Cor. 12:11). Weed out anything and everything that prevents You from employing Your gifts in me.

I open my life up to You that You would stir within me Your gifts of service: giving (Rom. 12:8), helping (1 Cor. 12:28), mercy (Rom. 12:6–8), and serving (1 Pet. 4:11).

Holy Spirit, free me to operate in Your gifts of power: healing, faith, and working of miracles (1 Cor. 12:9–10).

Move upon me in Your gifts of revelation: discernment (1 Cor. 12:10), evangelism (Eph. 4:11), exhortation (Rom. 12:8), tongues and interpretation of tongues (1 Cor. 12:10), word of knowledge (1 Cor. 12:8), and word of wisdom (1 Cor. 12:8).

Inspire in me Your gifts of influence and direction: administration (1 Cor. 12:28), apostleship and pastoring (Eph. 4:11), leadership and teaching (Rom. 12:7–8).

Most of all, move within me the gift of prophecy, that I would share Your life-giving words of edification, exhortation, and comfort to all people (1 Cor. 14:1–3). May I be heavenly focused and grounded in love, so my actions do not end up becoming meaningless pursuits (1 Cor. 13:1–3).

Although You never intended for me to flow in all the gifts at once, I avail myself to You to stir whatever gifts You desire within me. Make Your grace abound in me, so that in all things at all times, having all that I need, I will abound in every good work (2 Cor. 9:8).

See also:

1-4. Praising God for His Creation
2-4. Thanking God for His Grace and Mercy
2-7. Thanking God for Sending His Spirit
3-3. Bearing the Fruit of the Spirit
3-6. Learning Obedience
3-8. Joining God in His Will
5-8. Courage for Fear
10. Sickness and Disease
11-7. Outpouring of Signs and Wonders

5

PRODUCING ENDURANCE

> My brothers and sisters, whenever you face trials of any kind, consider it nothing but joy, because you know that the testing of your faith produces endurance; and let endurance have its full effect, so that you may be mature and complete, lacking in nothing. (James 1:2–4 NRSV)

Dear God, right now my life is so discouraging and confused that I feel like giving up . . . but I have nothing to give up *to*. Like a relentless storm, I'm pelted right and left by unforeseen forces intent on drawing me to my knees. In these moments of desperation my heart cries out:

> Whom have I in heaven but You?
> And there is none upon earth that I desire besides You.
> My flesh and my heart fail;
> But God is the strength of my heart and my portion forever.
> (Ps. 73:25–26 NKJV)

Lord God, You're my only hope. You are the strength of my heart and everything I will ever need.

When I consider the assorted lessons You work in my life, I realize that You are intent on developing endurance in me. You want me to remain steadfast when everyone around me is wilting under the pressure. When the day of evil comes You want me, having done everything, to stand (Eph. 6:13).

Therefore, Lord God, I take joy whenever I face trials of any kind, knowing that the testing of my faith produces endurance. I look forward to the day when Your work is done and I am mature and complete, lacking in nothing (James 1:2–4).

Jesus, You are the author and finisher of my faith (Heb. 12:2). Please protect my wearied faith in the palm of Your hand.

Regardless of the gale-force winds I encounter, I am determined to hold on to you with both hands. Your Word encourages me not to grow weary, because in due season *I will* reap a harvest if I do not lose heart (Gal. 6:9).

You give power to the weak and to those who have no might, You increase strength—You literally exchange Your strength with mine (Isa. 40:29)! I desperately need Your strength to continue. In my exhaustion, renew me like the eagle so I can run and not be weary; so I can walk and not faint (Isa. 40:31).

My greatest consolation is knowing You will never allow me to endure more than I can handle (Isa. 42:3). When I reach my breaking point You provide a way of escape (1 Cor. 10:13).

So I wait in patient expectation for Your divine intervention. I trust in Your goodness and wisdom, knowing You are creating me into the man (or woman) of God You desire me to be.

See also:

1-7. Adoring Christ, the Great "I AM"
1-10. Rejoicing in the Face of Discouragement
2-5. Thanking God for the Resurrection of Christ
3-9. Building Faith and Trust
4-8. Winning over Laziness
4-16. Fleeing Temptation
5-3. Hope for Despair

6

LEARNING OBEDIENCE

He who says, "I know Him," and does not keep His commandments, is a liar, and the truth is not in him. But whoever keeps His word, truly the love of God is perfected in him. By this we know that we are in Him. He who says he abides in Him ought himself also to walk just as He walked. (1 John 2:4–6 NKJV)

My endless platitudes and continual finger-pointing have worn thin. I have concluded that talking about obedience—especially in regard to other people—is much easier than living it. Lord, show me how to be a doer of the Word and not a hearer only (James 1:22).

Readily I admit that living according to my own desires is much more comfortable than living for You. Yet Your Word admonishes me that if I *really* love You, I'll keep Your commandments (John 14:21). My heart's desire is to grow in love and obedience. I don't want to be a liar by claiming to know You while walking in disregard to Your Word (1 John 2:4).

In my hard-hearted condition I so often wait until I'm dangling by the rope of my own selfishness before I cry out to You and change my ways. You died to free me from the clutches of sin; why should I return to a life of selfishness that only brings bondage? But I know that to obey is better than sacrifice (1 Sam. 15:22). Obedience means more to You than repentance.

Teach me how to walk in obedience. Do what it takes to make me clay in the hands of the Master Potter. Nothing in my life is sacred except my devotion to You; I place Your purposes above my preferences. Embed Your law in my mind and write it on my heart, so I will be led by my relationship with You rather than a list of dos and dont's (Jer. 31:33).

Lord God, show me what it means to die to my self just as Your Son Jesus did the night of His betrayal when He prayed, "Not My will, but Yours, be done" (Luke 22:42 NKJV). As a slave to righteousness I submit my will to Yours and dedicate myself to Your ways (Rom. 6:18). I commit myself to living according to Your Word and heeding the promptings of Your Holy Spirit (Ps. 81:11). *Completely*. Partial obedience is disobedience.

I will obey You, not for fear of reprisal or in pursuit of reward, but simply because I love You and I trust You. I acknowledge that it is You who works in me both to will and to do for Your good pleasure (Phil. 2:13). Thank You for giving me the power of Your Holy Spirit to follow through. Now I resolve to obey.

See also:

1-5. Acclaiming God's Majesty and the Beauty of Holiness
1-9. Loving God's Will
2-3. Thanking God for the Cross and the Blood
2-7. Thanking God for Sending His Spirit
3-1. Guarding Purity
3-2. Growing in Holiness
3-8. Joining God in His Will
3-9. Building Faith and Trust
4-13. Dying to Selfishness
11. Bringing in the Kingdom of God

7

DEVELOPING INTEGRITY

Likewise exhort the young men to be sober-minded, in all things showing yourself *to* be a pattern of good works; in doctrine showing integrity, reverence, incorruptibility, sound speech that cannot be condemned, that one who is an opponent may be ashamed, having nothing evil to say of you. (Titus 2:6–8 NKJV)

Righteous God, Your Word proclaims that You are not a man that You should lie, nor a son of man that You should change Your mind. What You say You *will* do. What You promise You *will* fulfill (Num. 23:19). Questioning the veracity of Your Word is unnecessary because You are the standard of integrity. Develop in me *Your* godly character. Give me a revelation of Your honesty, sincerity, and faithfulness that I would follow You in all Your ways.

Alert me when I am in danger of falling prey to subtle compromises. Even when I am about Your business, place a guard over my lips so I am not tempted to enhance the details or the extent of Your sovereign works. Stop me in the middle of my exaggerations; convict me when I resort to telling white lies; hold me to my commitments that my yes would be yes and my no would be no (Matt. 5:37). Make me a beacon of Your truth.

This day I make a covenant with my eyes, my hands, my ears, my thoughts, and my mouth that I won't entertain sin (Job 31:1). I will place no unclean thing before me. Steer me clear of sin even before I confront it. Grant me a healthy conscience, and place within me an inner alarm that sounds when encountering situations where my character may be in jeopardy. Help me recognize when I am weak, and give me the strength to do the right thing.

May my life be so unblemished and beyond reproach that what my family has to say about me is the same as my neighbors, coworkers, and You. I want to be the same person when I'm standing up in front of a crowd that I am when no one is looking. You see into my heart, knowing that the part of me that no one sees is the real me. I pray that my character and integrity would remind people of You.

My desire is for You to inquire about me as You did Job: "Have you considered My servant Job, that there is none like him on the earth, a blameless and upright man, one who fears God and shuns evil? And still he holds fast to his integrity" (Job 2:3 NKJV). When the waves of sin and destruction crash against me, I *will* remain true to You.

See also:

1-5. Acclaiming God's Majesty and the Beauty of Holiness
1-8. Worshiping in Spirit and Truth
2-3. Thanking God for the Cross and the Blood
2-6. Thanking God for Making Me the Righteousness of God in Christ
3-1. Guarding Purity
3-2. Growing in Holiness
4-14. Liberty from Lying and Deceit
5-5. Control for Panic
6-4. Financial Difficulties
11-6. Sound Judgment for Government and Public Officials

8

JOINING GOD IN HIS WILL

> In this manner, therefore, pray:
> Our Father in heaven,
> Hallowed be Your name.
> Your kingdom come.
> Your will be done
> On earth as it is in heaven.
> (Matt. 6:9–10 NKJV)

Lord Jesus, from the outset of Your ministry here on earth You were intent on fulfilling the will of Your Father in heaven. You did nothing on Your own, but You reached out in healing and with power only where You saw the Father already at work (John 5:19).

You taught us to pray to the Father, "Your kingdom come. / Your will be done / On earth as it is in heaven" (Matt. 6:10 NKJV).

The night You were betrayed, You prayed, "O My Father, if it is possible, let this cup pass from Me; nevertheless, not as I will, but as You will" (Matt. 26:39 NKJV). You set aside Your desire to bypass the cross in order to fulfill God's greater plan and die for my sins.

This day, I set aside *my* desires in order to join the Father in fulfilling His greater plan. *Father, not my will, but Yours be done.* I take my mind off myself and onto the Father's greater work. Like You, Lord Jesus, I can do nothing of myself. Please open my eyes to see what the Father is doing that I may join Him in His will.

Father God, thank You for giving me this wonderful tool of Your will called prayer. Quicken my spirit so I can pray into existence those things that are deepest in Your heart. In John 15:7 Jesus said, "If you abide in Me, and My words abide in you, you will ask what you desire, and it shall be done for you" (NKJV). I want to be so permeated in Jesus and His words that my prayers align with His will and ultimately Yours. Move me with the issues that are on Your heart so that whatever I bind on earth will be bound in heaven, and whatever I loose on earth will be loosed in heaven (Matt. 18:18).

I want to play an active part in Your kingdom's coming to earth. May my prayers and my actions contribute to seeing the kingdoms of this world become the kingdoms of our Lord and of His Christ (Rev. 11:15)!

See also:

1-9. Loving God's Will
1-10. Rejoicing in the Face of Discouragement
2-2. Thanking God for His Word
2-10. Thanking God for Choosing Me
3-4. Moving in the Gifts of the Spirit
3-6. Learning Obedience
3-9. Building Faith and Trust
4-3. Overcoming Pride
4-13. Dying to Selfishness
6-8. Direction for the Future
10. Sickness and Disease
11. Bringing in the Kingdom of God

9

BUILDING FAITH AND TRUST

But without faith it is impossible to please Him, for he who comes to God must believe that He is, and that He is a rewarder of those who diligently seek Him. (Heb. 11:6 NKJV)

Father God, my sincerest desire is to bring You pleasure—to hear You tell me at the end of the age, "Well done, My good and faithful servant" (Matt. 25:21 NKJV). Unless I am living by faith, I realize it is *impossible* to please You. So in all humility I come before You with this request: *Increase my faith*.

Reconfirm to me Your existence. Please give me the assurance that You exist beyond what I can feel or see (Heb. 11:1). Open my spiritual eyes so I can recognize the imprint of Your hand not only in world affairs, but also in the trivial nuances of my life (Matt. 6:25–32). Steer me away from the belief that I am the master of my own destiny so I don't relegate You to the status of a distant observer. Most of all, remind me that my salvation is eternally hidden in Jesus Christ, the author and finisher of my faith (Heb. 12:2).

Believing in Your existence is much easier than trusting in Your goodness. Lord God, I need a vision of the reward of faith. Instill within me the confidence that You are able and willing to intervene in my everyday affairs. Strengthen me so I can continue fervently in prayer until the object of my faith is secured. At the same time, place a watch over my eyes so that I focus not on the reward, but on You.

On my own I realize my inability to muster up a degree of faith even the size of a mustard seed. All faith begins with You for Your Word says, "Faith comes by hearing, and hearing by the word of

God" (Rom. 10:17 NKJV). Holy Spirit, speak into my heart the faith-creating words of God. Open my eyes to comprehend the depths of Your Word and my ears to recognize Your voice. And in my moments of doubt, heed my ambivalent cry, "Lord, I believe; help my unbelief!" (Mark 9:24 NKJV).

Redirect my eyes from the visible into the invisible (2 Cor. 5:7). Reinforce my shield of faith, so my trust in You is unshakable and so I can quench the fiery darts of the wicked one (Eph. 6:16). Show me the steps I should take because faith without works is dead (James 2:26).

"Some people trust the power of chariots or horses, / but [I] trust you, LORD God" (Ps. 20:7 CEV). Thank You that when my mind is stayed on You and I place my trust in You, You promise to keep me in perfect peace (Isa. 26:3). Lord God, You are in control.

See also:

1-2. Meditating on His Omnipotence and Omnipresence
1-9. Loving God's Will
1-10. Rejoicing in the Face of Discouragement
2-5. Thanking God for the Resurrection of Christ
2-7. Thanking God for Sending His Spirit
2-8. Thanking God for Supplying my Needs
2-9. Thanking God for His Protection
3-4. Moving in the Gifts of the Spirit
3-5. Producing Endurance
3-10. Finding Contentment
5-1. Rest for Sleeplessness
5-8. Courage for Fear
5-9. Redemption in the Face of Tribulation
10. Sickness and Disease
11. Bringing in the Kingdom of God

10

FINDING CONTENTMENT

Now godliness with contentment is great gain.
(1 Tim. 6:6 NKJV)

Maker of Heaven and Earth, my unceasing pursuits of self-gratification only result in continued emptiness. And my vain attempts to fill the hollow void inside only reinforce Your contention that the things of this world will never satisfy (Eccl. 2:4–11). You are *all*-sufficient, I am *de*ficient. Jesus, only You can fill the God-shaped hole in my life. You satisfy my longing soul with Your goodness (Ps. 107:9). Because You, Lord, are my Shepherd, I will never be in need (Ps. 23:1 CEV). Show me what it means to live in godliness and with contentment (1 Tim. 6:6).

I place at the foot of the cross my lust for more knowing, that what really matters doesn't reside in the temporal but in the eternal (2 Cor. 4:18). Therefore, I give to You my quest for personal fulfillment, happiness, riches, prestige, possessions, security, and leisure. I also offer to You the fruit of my discontent: complaining, grumbling, and ungratefulness. No longer do I choose to be weighed down by anything that detracts from knowing You. In their place, please fill me with Your love and compassion.

Reveal to me destructive habits that operate as substitutes for Your presence and the peace only You can give. Rather than being motivated out of fleshly cravings, guide my desires in accordance with Yours.

Because I trust in You, I know You are able to make all grace abound toward me, that I, always having all sufficiency in all things, may have an abundance for every good work (2 Cor. 9:8). I place my complete trust and confidence in Your abilities, knowing that all things are possible through Him who loved us (Phil. 4:13). Lord Jesus, affix my eyes onto the purposes of Your kingdom and the satisfaction that comes from knowing You.

See also:

1-3. Cherishing God's Love
1-6. Yearning for More of Jesus
2-6. Thanking God for Making Me the Righteousness of God in Christ
2-8. Thanking God for Supplying my Needs
3-9. Building Faith and Trust
4-6. Triumphing over Greed, Indulgence, and Materialism
4-9. Giving God Control of Selfish Ambition
5-2. Peace for Worry
9-7. Purpose in the Workplace
10-9. When God Doesn't Heal

4

SIN

When Jesus taught the disciples how to pray, He included the phrase, "Forgive us our debts [or trespasses, or sins] as we forgive our debtors" (Matt. 6:12 NKJV). When we give our lives to Christ, the Bible tells us that our sins are forgiven. "If we confess our sins, He is faithful and just to forgive us our sins and to cleanse us from all unrighteousness" (1 John 1:9 NKJV). Although we're forgiven, the battle with sin is far from over.

Even after we've given our lives to serving Jesus Christ, sin can continue to affect our walk with God. God spoke to Israel, His covenant children, in Isaiah 59:2, "But your iniquities have separated you from your God; / And your sins have hidden His face from you, / So that He will not hear" (NKJV). Before we are saved, our sins create a chasm between God and us that is impossible to cross except through the blood of Jesus Christ (Eph. 1:7). However, our sins can still separate us from God even after salvation. We may be headed to heaven, but we miss out on the fullness God intended for our lives. Never was the adage more true that confession is good for the soul.

Confessing our sins before God in prayer is like taking a shower before going on a date. You want to look good, and you definitely want to smell good! Unconfessed sin, on the other hand, makes us *self*-conscious. It's like going out on that same date sweaty and dirty. Not only is it embarrassing, but it's also repulsive to the party we're trying to impress. Beholding God's greatness and glory in our unclean condition causes us to respond as the prophet Isaiah did:

> Woe is me, for I am undone!
> Because I am a man of unclean lips,
> And I dwell in the midst of a people of unclean lips;
> For my eyes have seen the King, The LORD of hosts.
> (Isa. 6:5 NKJV)

We realize we are at the same time accepted, yet repulsive.

Without holiness, the writer of Hebrews reminded us, no one will see the Lord (Heb. 12:14). Fortunately, we can remove those filthy garments stained with sin and *come clean* with God. In the process, we ourselves are washed white as snow (Isa. 1:18). After we are cleansed, we become *God*-conscious. We sense the confidence to come boldly before the throne (Heb. 4:16). We share our heart with our heavenly Father, and if we take the time to listen, He shares His heart with us as well.

To begin this section, the Prayer of Salvation (the Sinner's Prayer) and the Prayer of Recommitment are included because the biggest deterrents to meeting God face-to-face are hearts that are uncommitted to Him.

1

THE PRAYER OF SALVATION (SINNER'S PRAYER)

For if you confess with your mouth that Jesus is Lord and believe in your heart that God raised him from the dead, you will be saved. (Rom. 10:9 NLT)

Dear Jesus,

I come before You and confess that I am a sinner (Rom. 3:23). There is no way that I could ever be good enough to save myself from spending eternity in hell (Rom. 6:23). But I thank You for dying on the cross in my place to pay the penalty for my sins (1 Peter 3:18).

Please forgive me for living by *my* rules. By confessing You as Lord I willfully and gladly give the controls of my life to You. I offer You all that I am that I would receive in return Your free gift of eternal life (Eph. 2:8–9).

Your resurrection from the dead proved once and forever that You are stronger than any power in the heavens or on earth (Rom. 8:38–39).

I hereby leave behind my previous life of sin and walk as a new creation in Jesus Christ (2 Cor. 5:17). Thank You for giving to me Your precious gift of eternal life.

See also:

1-3. Cherishing God's Love
1-7. Adoring Christ, the Great "I AM"
2-1. Thanking God for Sending Jesus

2-3. Thanking God for the Cross and the Blood
2-4. Thanking God for His Grace and Mercy
2-5. Thanking God for the Resurrection of Christ
2-6. Thanking God for Making Me the Righteousness of God in Christ
2-10. Thanking God for Choosing Me
3-9. Building Faith and Trust
6-9. Unsaved Spouse
7-4. For the Salvation of Your Child
11. Bringing in the Kingdom of God

2

THE PRAYER OF RECOMMITMENT

And the son said to him, "Father, I have sinned against heaven and in your sight, and am no longer worthy to be called your son." But the father said to his servants, "Bring out the best robe and put it on him, and put a ring on his hand and sandals on his feet. And bring the fatted calf here and kill it, and let us eat and be merry; for this my son was dead and is alive again; he was lost and is found." And they began to be merry. (Luke 15:21–24 NKJV)

Heavenly Father, I come before You with a sober and humble heart. I have feasted upon Your goodness, enjoyed Your presence, and yet have ventured away from Your protection and care. Father, I have sinned against heaven and in Your sight, and I am no longer worthy to be called Your child. I have tasted the fruit of my sin and found it bitter and unsatisfying.

At this moment I rely solely upon Your grace and mercy. Please forgive me for taking back the controls of my life and living as if You didn't exist. If there was a way I could earn Your reacceptance I would do it, but Your Word tells me, "The sacrifices of God are a broken spirit, / A broken and a contrite heart— / These, O God, You will not despise" (Ps. 51:17 NKJV).

So I come to You with a broken and contrite heart. Please cleanse me, renew me, and fill me once again. Take my heart of stone and transplant into me a heart of flesh; breathe new life into my weary spirit so I will follow You and walk in Your ways (Ezek. 36:26–27).

You could have given up on me but You didn't. Thank You for remaining faithful during my times of faithlessness (2 Tim. 2:13). Like the father of the prodigal son, You waited for me, yearning for my return. And then when You saw me, You came running.

Rather than bring condemnation, You have spared no expense to celebrate my return: You put a robe on my back, a ring on my hand, and You have killed the fatted calf (Luke 15:22–23). The only reason You take me back is because You love me with an everlasting love (Jer. 31:3). Thank You for loving me when I didn't love You in return, for wooing me back to the Father's heart when I tried to ignore the conviction of Your Holy Spirit.

In an attitude of repentance, I renounce my ways, I turn the opposite direction, and choose once again to follow You.

I commit to developing relationships with people who love You, to spending time with You, to remaining connected in a local body, and to sharing the good news of salvation with those around me.

Lord, You would rather that I be either hot or cold, but never lukewarm. Light Your fire in me that I would be hot for You (Rev. 3:15–16) so that all those around me would see the glory of Your presence.

See also:

1-3. Cherishing God's Love
1-8. Worshiping in Spirit and Truth
1-10. Rejoicing in the Face of Discouragement
2-3. Thanking God for the Cross and the Blood
2-4. Thanking God for His Grace and Mercy
3-8. Joining God in His Will
3-9. Building Faith and Trust
4-8. Winning over Laziness
11-1. Revival in the Church

3

OVERCOMING PRIDE

Likewise you younger people, submit yourselves to your elders. Yes, all of you be submissive to one another, and be clothed with humility, for "God resists the proud, / But gives grace to the humble." Therefore humble yourselves under the mighty hand of God, that He may exalt you in due time, casting all your care upon Him, for He cares for you. (1 Peter 5:5–7 NKJV)

Since our inception, men and women have wrestled with You for glory and control. I am no different. Professing to be wise, I so often become the fool and exchange the glory of the incorruptible God into my own corruptible image (Rom. 1:22–23). You have said, "You shall have no other gods before me" (Deut. 5:7 NKJV), yet I bow down to an idol of my own making and resemblance: me. Left to my own devices, I so easily worship the creature rather than the creator (Rom. 1:25).

The insidious tentacles of pride extend into every area of my life, seizing the opportunity to pry me away from You. Sovereign God, please forgive me for thinking more highly of myself than I should (Rom. 12:3). I realize that my struggle with pride strikes at the root of our relationship because steals from You what is rightfully Yours. You have said in Your Word that You will not allow anyone or anything to share in Your glory and praise (Isa. 42:8). You hate pride (Prov. 6:16–17a). And for that same sin Satan and his demons were cast out of heaven (Isa. 14:13–15).

I hesitate to even mention that the way You usually deal with pride is through divinely imposed acts of humility. "Pride goes before destruction, / And a haughty spirit before a fall" (Prov. 16:18 NKJV). But before I reach that point, I humbly come before You.

Please reveal to me those subtle and not-so-subtle areas of pride in my life. Show me when I become so caught up in my own self-importance that I raise myself above others and You. Convict me of those times when I don't think I need help from anyone . . . including You (2 Chron. 7:14). Grant me the sober judgment of myself to admit to others when I am wrong.

Search my heart and weed out areas of spiritual pride when I behave as if I have a corner on You. The danger of pride is that I can even become proud in my humility and take on the outward appearance while lacking the inward change. Any good work, any righteous act, any charitable contribution I perform that brings me glory rather than honor You is equivalent to filthy rags (Isa. 64:6). The only one I seek praise from is You (John 5:44)!

You resist the proud but give grace to the humble (1 Peter 5:5). I want to be a recipient of Your grace rather than an object of Your resistance. Therefore, I humble myself under Your mighty hand that You would exalt me in due time. Show me Your perspective of me so I would see myself as I really am—a sinner saved by grace.

I choose to clothe myself with humility. Please grant me the strength to follow through.

See also:

1-1. Magnifying the Lord
1-2. Meditating on His Omnipotence and Omnipresence
2-4. Thanking God for His Grace and Mercy
2-10. Thanking God for Choosing Me
3-2. Growing in Holiness
4-9. Giving God Control of Selfish Ambition

4

DELIVERANCE FROM SEXUAL PERVERSION

But among you there must not be even a hint of sexual immorality, or of any kind of impurity, or of greed, because these are improper for God's holy people. (Eph. 5:3 NIV)

"For the good that I will to do, I do not do; but the evil I will not to do, that I practice" (Rom. 7:19). Father God, I come to You in the name of Jesus and confess my struggle with sexual sin. I want to do the right thing, but somehow I keep falling back into my old destructive habits.

Please forgive me for seeking false intimacy through sexual perversion when I should be seeking You. Only You can fill the void in my life. I take full responsibility for my actions and repent—I go the opposite direction—of my sins.

Cleanse me of the grime that results from my sin and wipe away the memories of the past. "Create in me a clean heart, O God, / And renew a steadfast spirit within me. / Do not cast me away from Your presence, / And do not take Your Holy Spirit from me. / Restore to me the joy of Your salvation, / And uphold me by Your generous Spirit" (Ps. 51:10–12 NKJV). Return to me the innocence I once knew.

Unclean spirits of lust, pornography, fornication, adultery, homosexuality, and any other perverse sexual practice, I take authority over you and bind you in the name of Jesus. The enemy no longer has a foothold in my life. In its place I loose the manifest presence of Jesus Christ. I renounce all previous involvement in sexual perversion and put on the new man that God created, in righteousness and true holiness (Eph. 4:24).

I am washed, sanctified, and justified in the name of the Lord Jesus and by the Spirit of our God (1 Cor. 6:9–11). I put on the Lord Jesus Christ and make no provision for the flesh to fulfill its lusts (Rom. 13:14). My body is a temple of the Holy Spirit; I have been bought at a price, therefore I glorify God in my body and in my spirit, which belong to God (1 Cor. 6:19–20).

I have the mind of Christ (1 Cor. 2:16) and bring every thought into captivity to the obedience of Christ (2 Cor. 10:5). Henceforth I seek those things that are above, where Christ is, sitting at the right hand of God, and I set my mind on things above, not on things on the earth (Col. 3:1–2).

With my eyes I make a covenant that I will set nothing wicked before me (Job 31:1; Ps. 101:3). Lord God, give me the strength to steer my eyes away from sin. Place an alarm in my spirit to alert me of subtle temptation. Make all forms of sexual perversion repulsive to me. Most of all, give me the presence of mind to run from sin.

Bring me into redemptive relationships of accountability that will give me strength never to return. May You be glorified in me—body, mind, and spirit.

See also:

1-5. Acclaiming God's Majesty and the Beauty of Holiness
1-6. Yearning for More of Jesus
2-3. Thanking God for the Cross and the Blood
2-5. Thanking God for the Resurrection of Christ
3-1. Guarding Purity
3-2. Growing in Holiness
4-16. Fleeing Temptation

5

DEFEATING GOSSIP AND BACKBITING

Let no corrupt word proceed out of your mouth, but what is good for necessary edification, that it may impart grace to the hearers. (Eph. 4:29 NKJV)

God of all truth, I come before You and confess that I am guilty of murder. Although I may not kill in body, I do so in word. The barbs and knives in my speech have assassinated the character of others with precision.

You have spoken in Your Word that gossip is characteristic of a depraved mind just like murder, God-hating, and evildoing (Rom. 1:28-30) It tears apart the body of Christ, and when directed toward nonbelievers, it mars my testimony and draws people away from You.

Please forgive me for allowing bitterness and falsity to pass through the same lips that praise You (James 3:10). I have unwittingly played into the hand of Satan, the accuser of the brethren. The pain I have inflicted upon others ultimately pains You as well.

My inability to bridle my tongue has rendered my religion useless (James 1:26). Renew my faith so that my deeds align with my claims. Forgive me for giving license to gossip and backbiting by idly listening to the unkind words of others (Prov. 17:4). From this day forward, I resolve that my mouth *will not* sin (Ps. 17:3 NIV).

Worst of all, my gossip-mongering has affected my relationship with You. Your Word says that only those who speak the truth in their heart and refrain from backbiting may abide in Your tabernacle (Ps. 15:1–3). Lord Jesus, touch Your purifying coal to my lips and purge me of my sin (Isa. 6:7). I need to be restored to Your presence.

Remove from me the thrill of being "in the know." Give me the courage to shut gossip down when I hear it and to respond to people according to what I know is true. Free me from a poor view of myself that would seek to put others down in order to lift myself up. Rather than pass along *bad* news, transform me into one who shares *good* news. Guide my speech toward what is true, noble, just, pure, lovely, of good report, virtuous, and praiseworthy (Phil. 4:8). No longer will I rejoice in iniquity but in truth (1 Cor. 13:6).

Above all, season my speech with grace (Col. 4:6), so my words will be a tree of life and not a tool of death (Prov. 15:4). Fill me with Your love so that I, by nature, would edify and build up those around me. May this former gossip become a mouthpiece of Your love and mercy.

See also:

1-8. Worshiping in Spirit and Truth
2-2. Thanking God for His Word
2-6. Thanking God for Making Me the Righteousness of God in Christ
3-2. Growing in Holiness
3-3. Bearing the Fruit of the Spirit
8-2. Mending Broken Friendships
11-2. Sharing the Gospel

6

TRIUMPH OVER GREED, INDULGENCE, AND MATERIALISM

Do not love the world or the things in the world. If anyone loves the world, the love of the Father is not in him. For all that is in the world—the lust of the flesh, the lust of the eyes, and the pride of life—is not of the Father but is of the world. And the world is passing away, and the lust of it; but he who does the will of God abides forever. (1 John 2:15–17 NKJV)

Everywhere I go I am bombarded by external influences in the media—all seeking to seduce my fleshly desires. In a society transfixed on materialism and gain, Lord God, I want to be—I need to be—different. Lord, forgive me for allowing the world to force me into its mold. I don't want to be conformed to this world, so I ask for You to transform me by the renewing of my mind, that I would prove what is Your good and acceptable and perfect will (Rom. 12:2).

I don't want to be like the seed planted in the thorny ground who, after hearing the Word, was choked out by the cares of this world, the deceitfulness of riches, and the desires for other things. My concern for the things of this world will only make me unfruitful (Mark 4:18–19). Guide my eyes toward the things above.

You explicitly admonish in Scripture that Your people must not have even a *hint* of greed because it is improper for Your holy people (Eph. 5:3 NIV). The lust of the flesh, the lust of the eyes, and the pride of life are not of You but of this world, and my love for them proves that Your love is not in me. Jesus, cleanse me of my fleshly desires and renew my first love for You.

In the name of Jesus I will not lay up for myself treasures on earth, but I lay up for myself treasures in heaven. For where my treasure is, there my heart will be also (Matt. 6:19–21). Lord Jesus, *You are my treasure.* When I have You, I have every good thing (Ps. 34:10).

Deliver me from greed, indulgence, materialism and the lust for more. They will never satisfy like You do. But I will seek first Your kingdom and Your righteousness, knowing that all my needs—what I will eat, drink, and wear—will be met by You (Matt. 6:33). I want to seek You not for what You *can* give me, but for what You already *have* given me: forgiveness and eternal life through Jesus Christ.

Open my eyes to true reality that I would walk in the Spirit and not fulfill the lust of the flesh (Gal. 5:16).

Place in my heart a discontentment with this world and a longing for a better country (Heb. 11:16). Lord Jesus, I long for the day when I see You face-to-face.

I present my life to You as a living sacrifice (Rom. 12:1). My deepest desire is to know You, not only in the power of Your resurrection, but in the fellowship of Your sufferings, being conformed to Your death (Phil. 3:10). Examine my heart for any ulterior motives that would seek to manipulate You for selfish gain. Teach me what it means to be truly content (1 Tim 6:6).

Yet I realize that wealth and material possessions are not evil in themselves. Alert me when I begin seeking them rather than seeking You. Fill within me a heart of generosity that I would be a channel of Your blessing to others. Instill within me the joy of giving because You love cheerful—hilarious—givers (2 Cor. 9:7).

Lord God, thank You for holding nothing back when You gave Your Son Jesus to die on a cross for me. I likewise hold nothing back from You.

See also:

1-6. Yearning for More of Jesus
1-7. Adoring Christ, the Great "I AM"
2-4. Thanking God for His Grace and Mercy
2-8. Thanking God for Supplying my Needs
3-9. Building Faith and Trust
3-10. Finding Contentment
4-3. Overcoming Pride
4-7. Overpowering Envy and Jealousy
4-9. Giving God Control of Selfish Ambition
4-13. Dying to Selfishness
6-4. Financial Difficulties
11-3. Compassion for the Poor and Needy

7

OVERPOWERING ENVY AND JEALOUSY

For I was envious of the boastful,
When I saw the prosperity of the wicked . . .
When I thought how to understand this,
It was too painful for me—
Until I went into the sanctuary of God;
Then I understood their end.
(Ps. 73:3, 16–17 NKJV, italics added)

Almighty God, everything in heaven and on earth belongs to You, (Ps. 24:1) yet so often I behave as if, by divine right, they belong to me. I intensely desire those things that I do not have—falling prey to envy—and I clutch tightly onto those things that I fear of losing—succumbing to jealousy.

Please forgive me for allowing my fleshly passions to drive me to my knees and bow down to the idols of people, things, power, and control.

Your Word tells me "For where envy and self-seeking exist, confusion and every evil thing are there" (James 3:16 NKJV). The envy in my life has opened the door to confusion and every evil thing. My heartfelt desire is to close the door on any foothold Satan and the power of sin may have on my life. Please cleanse me and replace my envy with a yearning for more of You. "A heart at peace gives life to the body, / but envy rots the bones" (Prov. 14:30 NIV). Surround me with Your peace so I would trust You in my times of scarcity as well as abundance. Fill me with

Your love, knowing that love that comes from above is not envious (1 Cor. 13:4).

Your Word declares that jealousy is a work of the flesh and that those who practice such things will not inherit the kingdom of God (Gal. 5:19–21). Lord Jesus, replace my jealousy for the things of this world with a jealousy for You (Prov. 23:17). Convict me when I relegate You to second place, and create within me a passionate desire to stoke the fire of my love for You. Remind me that when I have You, I have nothing to fear because I have nothing to lose.

Today I make a declaration that I am putting on the Lord Jesus Christ and making no provision for the flesh, to fulfill its lusts (Rom. 13:13–14).

When I live according to my earthly perspective, I so easily become engulfed by the status of what I have and have not. Draw me into Your sanctuary and life-giving presence that I would live according to Your perspective (Ps. 73:17).

See also:

1-6. Yearning for More of Jesus
1-7. Adoring Christ, the Great "I AM"
2-4. Thanking God for His Grace and Mercy
2-8. Thanking God for Supplying my Needs
3-9. Building Faith and Trust
3-10. Finding Contentment
4-6. Triumphing over Greed, Indulgence, and Materialism
4-9. Giving God Control of Selfish Ambition
4-13. Dying to Selfishness

8

WINNING OVER LAZINESS

> And we desire that each one of you show the same diligence to the full assurance of hope until the end, that you do not become sluggish, but imitate those who through faith and patience inherit the promises. (Heb. 6:11–12 NKJV)

In this present age, the pressure is great to seek riches apart from the work of our hands, to do the minimum required. But, Lord God, Your Word exhorts me "And whatever you do, do it heartily, as to the Lord and not to men, knowing that from the Lord you will receive the reward of the inheritance; for you serve the Lord Christ" (Col. 3:23–24 NKJV).

Lord Jesus, because everything I do is dedicated to You, I am devoted to giving of myself completely to whatever task is at hand. You are the One I seek to bring pleasure.

Please forgive me for allowing myself to be mesmerized by a lack of purpose. I repent of my laziness and idleness and shake off the lethargy and doldrums that hinder me from accomplishing Your purposes.

"The steps of a good man are ordered by the LORD" (Ps. 37:23a NKJV). Give me a vision for where You desire to lead me and the strength to accomplish it. Through diligence and industriousness I commit myself to imitating those who through faith and patience inherit the promises (Heb. 6:12).

May the responsibility I model emanate into every area of my life: my job, my family, my friends, and most of all my relationship with You. Bless the fruit of my hands that my zeal for hard work—and for You—will shine as a testimony to all those around me of the difference You make.

See also:

1-2. Meditating on His Omnipotence and Omnipresence
1-9. Loving God's Will
2-1. Thanking God for Sending Jesus
2-5. Thanking God for the Resurrection of Christ
3-5. Producing Endurance
3-10. Finding Contentment
5-3. Hope for Despair
6-6. Time Struggles
6-8. Direction for the Future
11-9. Dispatching Laborers into the Field

9

GIVING GOD CONTROL OF SELFISH AMBITION

Do nothing out of selfish ambition or vain conceit, but in humility consider others better than yourselves. (Phil. 2:3 NIV)

Lord Jesus, You spoke "But I, when I am lifted up from the earth, will draw all men to myself" (John 12:32 NIV). With a repentant and contrite heart, I confess to You that rather than drawing people to You, I have sought to draw people to myself. Please forgive me for seeking power, control, and the esteem of others for selfish reasons.

Rather than trust You concerning my destiny, I have sought to wrest my future from Your hands. Teach me again what it means to walk in faith and trust, for without them I cannot please You (Heb. 11:6). I humble myself under Your mighty hand, that *You* would exalt me in due time, and cast all of my cares concerning my future upon You, because I know You care for me (1 Peter 5:6–7).

Forgive me for manipulating others in search of power and control. In the process I confess I have compromised my integrity. Alert my conscience when I unknowingly fall into old patterns of selfish ambition. Transform my cutting remarks into sincere words of encouragement and praise for those around me.

I have sought praise from others and become more concerned with what people think than what You think. From this day forward, I seek Your praise first and foremost (John 5:44). May I seek first Your kingdom and Your righteousness (Matt. 6:33).

In Your eyes selfish ambition is as serious as adultery, sorcery, and heresy, and those who practice such things will not inherit the kingdom of God (Gal. 5:19–21). By walking in selfish ambition, I have opened up my life to disorder and every evil practice (James 3:16 NIV).

With this in mind, I renounce my previous conduct and put on the Lord Jesus Christ making no provision for the flesh, to fulfill its lusts (Rom. 13:14). Wash me in the blood of the Lamb that I would be cleansed and made whole again (Rev. 7:14).

Restore my integrity, first in Your eyes, then in the eyes of those around me. May Your name be lifted up in my life so all men would be drawn to You.

See also:

1-8. Worshiping in Spirit and Truth
2-1. Thanking God for Sending Jesus
2-10. Thanking God for Choosing Me
3-3. Bearing the Fruit of the Spirit
3-7. Developing Integrity
3-8. Joining God in His Will
4-3. Overcoming Pride
4-6. Triumphing over Greed, Indulgence, and Materialism
4-7. Overpowering Envy and Jealousy
4-13. Dying to Selfishness
5-4. Order for Confusion
9. Job and Career

10

PREVAILING OVER ALCOHOL AND DRUGS

And do not be drunk with wine, in which is dissipation; but be filled with the Spirit. (Eph. 5:18 NKJV)

Lord God, I come to You in total helplessness. Drowning in my own lack of self-discipline, I reach out for You to save me.

I confess my addiction to sin, and I acknowledge You are the only one who can help me overcome it. Please forgive me for indulging in sorcery and seeking supernatural experiences apart from You. Cleanse me by the water of Your word (Eph. 5:26).

I have done a poor job of maintaining my control, so I give it to You. Bring me face-to-face with my addiction to these unhealthy habits and set me free from all bondages.

Spirits of sorcery and indulgence, I bind You in the name of Jesus. I belong to Jesus Christ—You no longer have authority over me. I renounce all rights and claims I have given to You and, by the power of Jesus Christ, I refrain from my alcohol (and/or drug) habit from this day forward. Jesus paid for my sins on the cross and purchased me so that I no longer need to walk in debt to sin (Gal. 1:4). Because I am in Christ, I am a new creation, the old has passed away; behold all things have become new (2 Cor. 5:17).

No temptation has overtaken me except such as is common to man; but God is faithful, who will not allow me to be tempted beyond what I am able, but with the temptation will also make the way of escape, that I may be able to bear it (1 Cor. 10:13).

Through the grace of Jesus Christ and the power of the Holy Spirit, I can withstand temptation. Lord, give me the eyes to identify temptation from a distance so I can flee from *it* and run to *You*.

"The name of the LORD is a strong tower; / The righteous run to it and are safe" (Prov. 18:10 NKJV). Lord Jesus, I hide myself in Your name and find safety from danger and evil. Shield me from attack. May Your strength be made perfect in my weakness (2 Cor. 12:9).

Heal the aches and pains that I have sought to numb through alcohol (and/or drugs). When I wept, You wept with me. When I felt rejected, You accepted me. Please reveal to me the depth of Your love and acceptance, and fill the void in my life that has gone so long unfilled.

Jesus, thank You that I don't have to fear condemnation from You (Rom. 8:1). Because You are the friend of sinners, I know You will look upon me with grace and mercy (Luke 7:34). Guide me into Your life-giving presence. Make me thirsty for more of You, and fill me up with the new wine of Your Holy Spirit.

Thank You for never giving up on me. Because You died for me, I'll live for You.

See also:

1-6. Yearning for More of Jesus
1-7. Adoring Christ, the Great "I AM"
2-3. Thanking God for the Cross and the Blood
2-4. Thanking God for His Grace and Mercy
3-5. Producing Endurance
4-1. The Prayer of Salvation (Sinner's Prayer)
4-2. The Prayer of Recommitment
4-16. Fleeing Temptation
10-5. Emotional Healing

11

LETTING GO OF BITTERNESS AND UNFORGIVENESS

And be kind to one another, tenderhearted, forgiving one another, even as God in Christ forgave you. (Eph. 4:32 NKJV)

Lord Jesus, You promised that in this world we would have tribulation (John 16:33). Never did You promise that we would elude troubles and injustice.

I confess to You that the injustices perpetrated upon me still ache deep within my soul. The unforgiveness in my life works like a cancer, slowly eating away what spiritual vitality I have.

Please forgive me for walking in unforgiveness. My refusal to forgive only cheapens the debt You paid on my behalf to forgive my sins. I realize my refusal to forgive affects my relationship with You as well as those who have harmed me (Matt. 6:14–15). Lord, I don't want to be like the servant who was forgiven an enormous debt only to turn around and refuse to forgive another man of a pittance (Matt. 18:21–35).

In the world's greatest act of injustice, You were nailed to a cross on false charges. I may have been wronged, but You suffered a far greater wrong. Yet hanging on the cross You cried out, "Father, forgive them; for they know not what they do" (Luke 23:34 KJV). Instill within me the kind of love that releases people from their debt of offense.

So this day, I release to You the debts I have held over the heads of those who have wronged me. Forgive me of my debts as I now forgive my debtors (Matt. 6:12). And may my only remaining debt be a debt of love, even to those who have hurt me (Rom. 13:8).

Liberate me from my bondage to unforgiveness and bitterness. I want no part of anything that hinders my walk with You. Remove any cancerous root of bitterness, and heal the hurts buried deep inside with the balm of Your Holy Spirit. I choose to change the attitude of my heart toward those who have wronged me so I can forgive them *from my heart* (Matt. 18:35). Please wipe away the memories that recount the injustices from the past and give me discernment to avoid needless hurt and pain in the future.

Whenever those weeds of unforgiveness and bitterness surface, show me that You love my offenders as much as You love me. Remind me that even in those times when I have wronged You and sinned against You, You still love me, accept me, and welcome me into Your arms.

Therefore, I leave the offenses of the past behind and clothe myself with Your love (Col. 3:12–14).

See also:

1-6. Yearning for More of Jesus
1-10. Rejoicing in the Face of Discouragement
2-3. Thanking God for the Cross and the Blood
2-4. Thanking God for His Grace and Mercy
3-2. Growing in Holiness
3-3. Bearing the Fruit of the Spirit
4-12. Victory over Hatred
5-6. Calmness for Anger and Rage
8. Relationships
10-5. Emotional Healing
11-4. Unity in the Body of Christ

12

VICTORY OVER HATRED

If someone says, "I love God," and hates his brother, he is a liar; for he who does not love his brother whom he has seen, how can he love God whom he has not seen? And this commandment we have from Him: that he who loves God must love his brother also. (1 John 4:20–21 NKJV)

Loving heavenly Father, I am a man [or woman] of unclean hands. My venomous words and destructive thoughts incriminate me of murder. Bitterness and unforgiveness rage so uncontrollably in my life that I can no longer contain it. My claim of devotion to You while stewing in hatred toward my neighbor has turned my faith into a farce. So I come before You in need of Your divine intervention.

You have clearly spoken in Your Word, "Whoever hates his brother is a murderer, and you know that no murderer has eternal life abiding in him" (1 John 3:15 NKJV). I realize that the hatred I have harbored toward those who have hurt me makes me liable for eternal destruction. With a sober spirit I humbly ask Your forgiveness for allowing hate to control me. Only through the blood of Your forgiveness can I be restored to a right relationship with You.

Through enmity and resentment I have given the power of control to my *perceived* enemy and *the* Enemy. In the name of Jesus, I repent of my destructive behavior, and from this day forward, I place the control of my life into Your hands.

Awake me in those times when I deny the hatred festering in my heart yet through my actions prove that it still exists.

Jesus, I release the burden of retaliation into Your charge for Your Word says, "Vengeance is Mine, I will repay" (Rom. 12:19 NKJV). With my mouth and in my heart I ask that You would bless those who have hurt me, maligned me, and sought my destruction. With my confession I heap coals of fire on his (or her) head that he (or she) would come under the conviction of the Holy Spirit and brought to repentance and restoration.

There is no way I can love this person on my own; I need an impartation of Your *agape* love. Fill me with the love You have for my brother (or sister) and grant me the humility and courage to initiate our reconciliation. May the testimony of our love in the face of hatred point people to Your all-consuming, all-forgiving love (Heb. 12:14–15).

See also:

1-3. Cherishing God's Love
1-10. Rejoicing in the Face of Discouragement
2-3. Thanking God for the Cross and the Blood
2-4. Thanking God for His Grace and Mercy
3-3. Bearing the Fruit of the Spirit
4-11. Letting Go of Bitterness and Unforgiveness
5-6. Calmness for Anger and Rage
6-3. Conflict Between Husband and Wife
8. Relationships
10-5. Emotional Healing
11-4. Unity in the Body of Christ

13

DYING TO SELFISHNESS

For where envy and self-seeking *exist,* confusion and every evil thing are there. (James 3:16 NKJV)

Merciful God, everywhere I go I am confronted by a society increasingly fixated with self. The allure of self-gratification in this world feeds on fleshly desires already primed for fulfillment. Yet Your Word exhorts me:

> "You shall love the LORD your God with all your heart, with all your soul, and with all your mind." This is the first and great commandment. And the second is like it: "You shall love your neighbor as yourself." (Matt. 22:37 NKJV)

I understand Your desire for my undivided love, and that my love for You is proven by the way I love others. A part of me wants to do Your will, and yet another part of me wants to live for myself. Where can I go to be delivered from this bondage? "Who will deliver me from this body of death?" (Rom. 7:24 NKJV).

Jesus, only You can deliver me. I have placed my pleasures over Your priorities. In my state of selfishness there is no way Your love can be found in me because love doesn't seek its own (1 Cor. 13:5). Please forgive me for living in selfishness. Cleanse me, wash me anew, and clothe me with Your robe of righteousness (Isa. 61:10).

There is nothing redemptive in my flesh's insatiable thirst for more, so I ask for Your power to kill it. "And those who are Christ's have crucified the flesh with its passions and desires" (Gal. 5:24 NKJV). You died on the cross to deliver me from the penalty of sin and selfishness. Make my fleshly desires repulsive, and make Your will my greatest longing.

Reveal to me those fleshly desires in my life that masquerade under the appearance of righteousness, and convict me when I try to make You a manipulative tool of my own selfishness. Deliver me from the romantic notion of dying to self. Rather than talk about it, grant me the grace to live it. I place my narcissistic cravings on the altar that You would give Your life to me. Move me out of my comfort zones and into the exhilarating walk of the Spirit (Gal. 5:16).

In place of my selfishness, fill the void with a love for others borne out of an insatiable love for You. Transform my selfishness into servanthood (1 Cor. 9:19), and place within me the sincere desire to seek the well-being of others (1 Cor. 10:24).

Above all, may my heart be fixated on Your will. May *Your* kingdom come and *Your* will be done in my life as it is in heaven (Matt. 6:10).

See also:

1-6. Yearning for More of Jesus
1-7. Adoring Christ, the Great "I AM"
2-1. Thanking God for Sending Jesus
2-3. Thanking God for the Cross and the Blood
3-8. Joining God in His Will
4-3. Overcoming Pride
4-6. Triumphing over Greed, Indulgence, and Materialism
4-9. Giving God Control of Selfish Ambition
6-3. Conflict Between Husband and Wife
11. Bringing in the Kingdom of God

14

LIBERTY FROM LYING AND DECEIT

Do not lie to one another, since you have put off the old man with his deeds, and have put on the new man who is renewed in knowledge according to the image of Him who created him. (Col. 3:9–10 NKJV)

Lord God, the webs of deception I have spun have at last entangled me. Caught in the mire of my sin, I am now confronted by the seriousness of my behavior. Lying and deceit have crept into my speech, and in the process, Your truth—and my integrity—have been compromised.

Please forgive me for allowing white lies, exaggeration, dishonesty, and deceit into my life. They have no place in Your kingdom and in Your eyes, they are utterly detestable (Prov. 6:16). I recognize that regardless of whom I am lying to, I am ultimately lying to You (Acts 5:3). Forgive my rationalizations for allowing their practice to continue unabated. My acceptance of this sin only lessens the importance of truth and integrity. I have unwittingly become a mouthpiece of the father of lies.

Satan is a liar, devoid of truth, and lying is his native language (John 8:44 NIV). So I rebuke him in Jesus' name; his lies have no place in my life.

Spirits of deceit (1 Tim. 4:1), and lying, I forbid you to have any further influence on me. I renounce all previous entanglements and associations with you and place myself under the blood-stained cross of Jesus Christ. I break off all generational spirits of lying and deceit that have been passed down to me and I come against them in the name of Jesus that "at the name of Jesus every knee should bow, of those in heaven, and of those on earth, and of those under the earth, and that every tongue should confess that Jesus Christ is Lord, to the glory of God the Father" (Phil. 2:10–11 NKJV). With my tongue I confess that Jesus Christ is Lord.

"As long as my breath is in me, / And the breath of God in my nostrils, / My lips will not speak wickedness, / Nor my tongue utter deceit" (Job 27:3 NKJV).

Lord God, I realize that my dishonesty strikes at the root of my relationship with You and with others. Forge my character in the refining fire of Your holiness so I can earn Your trust once again. Reveal to me the people with whom I need to make amends and give me the courage to confess my sin.

Remove from me the illusion that truth and falsity are compatible and revive in me a love for Your truth (2 Thess. 2:10). May my yes be yes and my no be no (Matt. 5:37). Holy Spirit, stop me in the middle of even the slightest falsehood and free me from this compulsion that causes me to be deceitful even when I don't intend to. I seek to be led by the Spirit in order that I won't fulfill the lusts of the flesh (Gal. 5:16).

Awaken my slumbering conscience so I can live in integrity and enjoy the pleasures of Your life-giving presence (Ps. 15:1,2). Lord Jesus, my heart's desire is to walk in Your truth (Ps. 86:11).

See also:

1-5. Acclaiming God's Majesty and the Beauty of Holiness
1-8. Worshiping in Spirit and Truth
2-2. Thanking God for His Word
3-2. Growing in Holiness
3-3. Bearing the Fruit of the Spirit
3-7. Developing Integrity
4-16. Fleeing Temptation

15

FINDING FREEDOM FROM REBELLION

> All we like sheep have gone astray;
> We have turned, every one, to his own way;
> And the LORD has laid on Him the iniquity of us all.
> (Isa. 53:6 NKJV)

Lord Jesus, although I claim to be Your disciple—a follower of You—I have wandered off on my own. Attempting to master my own destiny, my digression has only reaped a hardened heart toward You. By seeking my own path I have exposed myself to Your wrath (Deut. 9:7) and have succeeded in losing my way. Professing to be wise, I have become a fool (Rom. 1:22).

I repent of my sin of rebellion. With a heavy heart I acknowledge that my rebellion is like witchcraft because I have usurped Your authority for my own benefit (1 Sam. 15:23). Forsaking all other authorities, I have become a law unto myself. I acknowledge that by refusing to walk in submission to those You have placed over me, I am rebelling against You as well (Num. 16:1–11). In the process, I have grieved Your Holy Spirit and become an unwitting enemy of the very one I claim to follow: You. (Isa. 63:10).

Please forgive me for my pride, arrogance, and self-sufficiency. Release me from the bondage to my self-serving desires (Neh. 9:17). If You lived as independent of me as I have attempted of You, I wouldn't even exist. More important than protecting my "rights" is doing the "right thing," so I change allegiances and make my *declaration of dependence* upon You.

Soften my hardened heart but don't break my spirit. In a society that glorifies the rebel, even without a cause, I willingly choose to humble myself, taking the form of a servant (Phil. 2:5–7). Uncover any motives that seek to cloak my rebellion in "God and me" terms. Turn my rugged individualism into a tenacious commitment to serving You *and* others. May I become *one* functioning member of a body of believers, reliant upon one another, and together, reliant upon You.

See also:

1-1. Magnifying the Lord
1-2. Meditating on His Omnipotence and Omnipresence
1-9. Loving God's Will
2-10. Thanking God for Choosing Me
3-8. Joining God in His Will
4-3. Overcoming Pride
4-9. Giving God Control of Selfish Ambition
4-13. Dying to Selfishness
7-3. When Your Child Is Rebellious
9-3. Problems with Your Boss
11-4. Unity in the Body of Christ

16

FLEEING TEMPTATION

For we do not have a High Priest who cannot sympathize with our weaknesses, but was in all points tempted as we are, *yet* without sin. Let us therefore come boldly to the throne of grace, that we may obtain mercy and find grace to help in time of need. (Heb. 4:15–16 NKJV)

Dear Lord Jesus, there is no way I can withstand the allure of temptation on my own. The ambivalent feelings I sense inside have neutralized my resistance. My flesh craves gratification, while my spirit cries out for more of You. This war fought on the battleground of my soul—my mind, will, and emotions—will be won only as my spirit works in partnership with Your Holy Spirit.

You told Your disciples, "Watch and pray, lest you enter into temptation. The spirit indeed is willing, but the flesh is weak" (Matt. 26:41 NKJV). I come before You in prayer with a willing spirit and my flesh raging out of control. I'm sorry and I repent for allowing myself to be consumed with sin. Please wash me with Your cleansing blood of forgiveness, so I can be restored to You and set free from the entanglements of my sinful nature.

I thank You that I can come to You with boldness, knowing that You truly identify with my struggles; You were tempted in the very same ways as I am, yet You resisted the attraction—and consequences—of sin. Flood my life with Your mercy and grace in this time of need (Heb. 4:16). In my weakness, be made strong (2 Cor. 12:10).

Satan, You have come only to steal, kill, and destroy. But Jesus came that I may have life and have it more abundantly (John 10:10). Therefore, I put on the armor of God—my helmet of salvation, my breastplate of righteousness, my belt of truth, my shoes of the preparation of the gospel of peace, my shield of faith, and my sword of the Spirit, which is the Word of God—so I can quench your fiery darts (Eph. 6:11–17). I rebuke You and command You by the authority of the name of Jesus Christ to cease your enticements.

By the power of the Holy Spirit I *will* abstain from every form of evil (1 Thess. 5:22). I stand on God's faithful promise: "No temptation has overtaken you except such as is common to man; but God is faithful, who will not allow you to be tempted beyond what you are able, but with the temptation will also make the way of escape, that you may be able to bear it" (1 Cor. 10:13 NKJV). Lord God, reveal to me Your strategy for my escape. Alert me before I face any compromising situations that feed on my weaknesses. Give me such a strong sense of the seriousness of sin that I would be compelled to run away from even the slightest hint of compromise and run into Your arms of love.

In all earnestness I admit I cannot do this on my own; please bring me into relationships of trust and accountability with godly people who will encourage me in my struggle against sin.

Please grant me the *hindsight* to recall earlier times when I mistakenly trusted in my own strength; the *foresight* to recognize and change the patterns that cause me to repeat the same sinful habits; and the *insight* to realize that apart from the power of Your Holy Spirit, I cannot live the life of holiness You call me to.

Give me eyes to see that the temptation of my flesh is also the testing of my faith. To the extent I succeed will determine the consequences of my sin—further separation from God (Isa. 59:2), or the rewards of my endurance: character and maturity (Rom. 5:3–5).

Your divine power has given me everything I need for life and godliness through my knowledge of You who called me by Your own glory and goodness. Through these You have given me Your very great and precious promises, so that through them I may participate in the divine nature and escape the corruption in the world caused by my evil desires (2 Peter 1:3 NIV). Thank You for imparting to me Your divine power to live the life that transcends my sinful nature.

See also:

1-1. Magnifying the Lord
1-2. Meditating on His Omnipotence and Omnipresence
1-5. Acclaiming God's Majesty and the Beauty of Holiness
1-6. Yearning for More of Jesus
1-10. Rejoicing in the Face of Discouragement
2-3. Thanking God for the Cross and the Blood
2-5. Thanking God for the Resurrection of Christ
2-7. Thanking God for Sending His Spirit
3-1. Guarding Purity
3-2. Growing in Holiness
3-3. Bearing the Fruit of the Spirit
3-7. Developing Integrity
3-10. Finding Contentment
4. Sin

5

STRESS

We aren't sure whether he was just having a bad day or perhaps an adversary of his—one not devoted to Yahweh—was enjoying recent success. Nevertheless, Asaph, a psalmist in the temple courts under King David and King Solomon, brought his complaints before God. Instead of asking, "Why do bad things happen to good people?" he turned the question around and asked, "Why do good things happen to bad people?"

Have you ever asked God the same question, perhaps after a coworker of inferior morals or ability gets the promotion you felt you deserved? Let's eavesdrop for a moment to see whether you can identify with Asaph's lament:

> Surely God is good to Israel,
>   to those who are pure in heart.
> But as for me, my feet had almost slipped;
>   I had nearly lost my foothold.
> For I envied the arrogant
>   when I saw the prosperity of the wicked.

They have no struggles;
  their bodies are healthy and strong.
They are free from the burdens common to man;
they are not plagued by human ills . . .
This is what the wicked are like—
  always carefree, they increase in wealth.
Surely in vain have I kept my heart pure;
  in vain have I washed my hands in innocence.
All day long I have been plagued;
  I have been punished every morning.
If I had said, "I will speak thus,"
  I would have betrayed your children.
When I tried to understand all this,
  it was oppressive to me.
(Ps. 73:1–5, 12–16 NIV)

Observing the wicked flourishing in contrast to the fruitless strivings of the righteous was more than Asaph could bear. "Surely in vain have I kept my heart pure." What's the use of serving God when those who could care less about Him seem to flourish while those who do care, don't? Regardless of the level of spiritual maturity, we have all experienced seasons where we questioned the mystery of God's goodness and justice.

How we feel colors our perspective. Our perception—at least to us—becomes reality. On the heels of his greatest triumph in ministry, Elijah felt so distraught that he asked God to take him to his eternal home (1 Kings 19). In his own eyes, with Queen Jezebel placing a death warrant over his head, his ministry was over. In God's eyes, Elijah's most fruitful ministry lay ahead. What Elijah encountered next on the side of Mt. Horeb is what Asaph referred to in the following verse:

> Till I entered the sanctuary of God;
> then I understood their final destiny.
> (Ps. 73:17 NIV)

Not until Asaph encountered the life-giving presence of God could he evaluate the destiny of the righteous and the wicked. *God's presence brings perspective.* When we enter into the sanctuary of God through prayer, we see our life not from the temporal point of view but the eternal.

The glory of prayer is that we can be ourselves in God's presence. He doesn't want us to deny our feelings. Asaph didn't. Elijah didn't. Jesus surely didn't (Matt. 26:38–42). We can share our greatest disappointments, our deepest hurts . . . and He can handle it! In fact, only when we give Him who we really are, is He able to give us who He really is. That's when God moves our mountains of stress and emotions.

1

REST FOR SLEEPLESSNESS

Unless the LORD builds the house,
They labor in vain who build it;
Unless the LORD guards the city,
The watchman stays awake in vain.
It is vain for you to rise up early,
To sit up late,
To eat the bread of sorrows;
For so He gives His beloved sleep.
(Ps. 127:1–2 NKJV, italics added)

Dear Lord, my body is tired, my soul is weary. The fatigue I feel affects everything I do: my work, my emotions, my relationships, my walk with You. More than just sleep, I need the rest only You can give.

Your Word promises, "There remains therefore a rest for the people of God" (Heb. 4:9 NKJV). As one of Your children, I ask that You would lift me out of my restlessness and into Your quiet repose. Carry me to a place of rest from my labor just as You did on the seventh day of creation (Heb. 4:10).

In the name of Jesus, I take every thought captive to the obedience of Christ (2 Cor. 10:5 NASB). "For God has not given us a spirit of fear, but of power and of love and of a sound mind" (2 Tim. 1:7 NKJV). I pull out all roots of anger, anxiety, and tension that would wreak havoc with my mind. Lord, only Your strength can bring my frenzied thoughts to a standstill. Surround me with an impenetrable fortress to ward off any cares or concerns that don't begin with You.

And in those moments of wakefulness, bring to my remembrance the many stories of Your faithfulness and love both from Your Word and in my life (Ps. 92:2). Redeem my time awake that I may meditate on Your Word (Ps. 119:148), intercede for others (2 Tim. 1:3), and enjoy Your presence (Ps.27:4).

Relax my muscles. Muffle all the distractions that hover around me. Give me a song in the night that I would dwell in Your presence even in my sleep (Ps. 42:8). "I will both lie down in peace, and sleep; / For You alone, O LORD, make me dwell in safety" (Ps. 4:8 NKJV).

And when I awaken, dear God, reinvigorate me with Your strength not only to face another day, but to walk in the victory Your Son Jesus won at Calvary.

See also:

1-3. Cherishing God's Love
2-8. Thanking God for Supplying My Needs
2-9. Thanking God for His Protection
3-9. Building Faith and Trust
5-2. Peace for Worry
5-5. Control for Panic
5-8. Courage for Fear
6-8. Direction for the Future
7. The Lives of Your Children
8. Relationships
9. Job and Career

2

PEACE FOR WORRY

Be anxious for nothing, but in everything by prayer and supplication, with thanksgiving, let your requests be made known to God; and the peace of God, which surpasses all understanding, will guard your hearts and minds through Christ Jesus. (Phil 4:6–7)

Lord Jesus, I haven't done a very good job serving as my own messiah, much less the savior of this world, so I give back what rightfully belongs to You. Please forgive me for allowing worry and anxiety to take root in my life.

By worrying, I have displayed an obvious lack of faith. And without faith it is impossible to please You (Heb. 11:6). Forgive me for living from a worldly perspective rather than Your eternal perspective.

Your yoke is easy, and Your burden is light (Matt. 11:30). I give You the weight of the world that I have taken on my shoulders, and I place it in Your hands; I cast all my cares upon You, because You care for me (1 Peter 5:7).

Anxious and worrisome thoughts, I bind you in the name of Jesus. I take every thought captive to the obedience of Christ (2 Cor. 10:5). And in its place I loose the peace of God, which surpasses all understanding, that it would guard my heart and mind through Christ Jesus (Phil. 4:7).

"You will keep him in perfect peace, / Whose mind is stayed on You, / Because he trusts in You" (Isa. 26:3 NKJV). I make this declaration: I will fix my thoughts on You because I trust in You. I will say of the LORD, You are my refuge and my fortress; My God, in whom I will trust (Ps. 91:2). You are in complete control, and You are greater than any fear my mind can conceive.

I cannot change the future; I cannot change human hearts; but my situation can be changed as I bring my concerns before You. Teach me what it means to be persevering in prayer. Transform my worry into a rock-solid faith that cannot be moved. "When my heart is overwhelmed; / Lead me to the rock that is higher than I" (Ps. 61:2 NKJV).

Make me like the tree planted by the waters, which spreads out its roots by the river so that when hardships come, my leaves will be green. Even in the year of drought, I *will* yield fruit because my trust is in You alone (Jer. 17:7–8).

See also:

1-1. Magnifying the Lord
1-2. Meditating on His Omnipotence and Omnipresence
1-7. Adoring Christ, the Great "I AM"
2-5. Thanking God for the Resurrection of Christ
2-8. Thanking God for Supplying my Needs
3-9. Building Faith and Trust
3-10. Finding Contentment
5-4. Order for Confusion
5-5. Control for Panic
5-8. Courage for Fear

3

HOPE FOR DESPAIR

> Why are you downcast, O my soul?
> Why so disturbed within me?
> Put your hope in God,
> for I will yet praise him,
> my Savior and my God. (Ps. 42:5–6a NIV)

Lord God, I feel enveloped in darkness and despair. *Who do I turn to? Where do I go from here?* If I could give up, I would, but I have nothing to give up *to*. So in this dark hour, I hold fast to You. I will not let go of the hope I have in You because You are my only hope (Ps. 39:7). I rest myself completely in Your goodness, faithfulness, and love.

Just because I can't see You doesn't mean You aren't *already* at work in my life. I cling tenaciously to the promise in Your word:

> We know that all things work together for good to those who love God, to those who are the called according to His purpose. (Rom. 8:28 NKJV)

With confidence I can say that You are working everything together for good. Therefore, I will *not* be downcast. I will *not* be disturbed within. I will place my hope in God, and I look forward to the day when I will praise You for the fulfillment of Your promises (Ps. 42:5). My hope rests solidly in you (Ps. 39:7) and not in the problems or emotions I encounter. Greater is He who is in me than He who is in the world (1 John 4:4).

You redeem my life from the pit and crown me with love and compassion (Ps. 103:4). You can redeem even my despair:

> Not only that, but we also glory in tribulations, knowing that tribulation produces perseverance; and perseverance, character; and character, hope. Now hope does not disappoint, because the love of God has been poured out in our hearts by the Holy Spirit who was given to us. (Rom. 5:3–5 NKJV)

Lord God, when my hope is in You, I can't help but draw closer to You; I can't help but grow deeper in maturity; I can't help but sense a greater outpouring of Your Holy Spirit in my life. Open my eyes to the eternal lessons You are teaching me (Rom. 15:4).

Lord, I don't want to live in denial of what I face, yet I know I should walk by faith and not by sight (2 Cor. 5:7). Please give me a vision of You standing with me in the middle of my despair. Lift me out of the muck and mire and into the heavenly places and clothe me with the garment of praise for the spirit of heaviness (Isa. 61:3).

Dispel the clouds of discouragement that encompass me. I know that Your desire is to free me from my discouragement because Your yoke is easy and Your burden is light (Matt. 11:30).

See also:

1-1. Magnifying the Lord
1-10. Rejoicing in the Face of Discouragement
2-5. Thanking God for the Resurrection of Christ
2-8. Thanking God for Supplying my Needs
3-5. Producing Endurance
3-9. Building Faith and Trust
5-9. Redemption in the face of Tribulation

4

ORDER FOR CONFUSION

For God is not the author of confusion but of peace, as in all the churches of the saints. (1 Cor. 14:33 NKJV)

Lord Jesus, Your Word assures me that if I lack wisdom, I can ask of You and You will give it liberally and without reproach when I ask in faith (James 1:5–6). Please grant me the wisdom that comes from above and clarity to my perspective so I can make godly decisions.

You are not the author of confusion but rather the God of peace and order (1 Cor. 14:40). Just as You stood over the formless void at the beginning of creation and fashioned the heavens and the earth, I ask that You would preside over the formless void before me and create order (Gen. 1:2). Bring clarity to my clutter and coherence to my confusion. I glory in the fact that You do Your best work with chaos!

Examine my heart and purge me of any selfishness because "where envy and self-seeking exist, confusion and every evil thing are there" (James 3:16 NKJV).

Satan, you are the author of confusion. I forbid you to bring any more disorder into my life. I renounce your work and tell you: "In the name of Jesus, remove your influences from my affairs." I speak to the disarray and disorder and tell you to align yourselves with the perfect will of God (Rom. 12:2). My steps are ordered by the Lord (Prov. 20:24).

At the same time, dear God, I admit that Your ways aren't

necessarily neat and tidy. Your ways are higher than my ways and Your thoughts higher than my thoughts (Isa. 55:9). You work far beyond what I can see or understand. Please grant me the discernment to distinguish between Your ways, my ways, and the ways of the enemy.

Align my plans with Your will. Give me the confidence to know beyond a shadow of a doubt that You are the one leading me forward.

See also:

1-9. Loving God's Will
2-2. Thanking God for His Word
3-8. Joining God in His Will
5-5. Control for Panic
6-4. Financial Difficulties
6-8. Direction for the Future
9-1. Wisdom and Guidance in Your Job Search

5

CONTROL FOR PANIC

For God has not given us a spirit of fear, but of power and of love and of a sound mind. (2 Tim. 1:7 NKJV)

Lord God, when everything in my life goes according to plan, walking by faith and waiting upon You isn't so difficult. But right now the temptation to move ahead of You is great. The suddenness of this storm propels me to react out of desperation rather than faith.

I know that responding in panic and moving ahead of You only leads me out of Your blessing and into poverty (Prov. 21:5) and sin (Prov. 19:2). But everything within me screams to do something. Now. By Your mercy and grace, show me that by jumping ship I am only diving into the turbulent and uncertain waters below.

You have not given me a spirit of fear, but of power, love, and a sound mind (2 Tim. 1:7). During this moment of distress I need an infusion of Your power and a reaffirmation of Your steadfast love. Please bring to a halt the furious thoughts that race in my head. Give me the presence of mind to be still and know that You are God (Ps. 46:10). "Truly my soul silently waits for God; / From Him comes my salvation. / He only is my rock and my salvation; / He is my defense; / I shall not be greatly moved" (Ps. 62:1–2 NKJV).

My passions will not run away from me, nor will I respond out of self-preservation. Holy Spirit, I bring my thoughts, my emotions, my words, and my actions under Your control. Lead me by Your Spirit, and stop me before I move ahead of You. Please quicken my spirit to hear Your voice so I can rest in Your assurance that even the wind and the raging sea obey You (Mark 4:41). Open my eyes to see that You are as near to me in my turmoil as You are when everything is at peace. I want to walk by faith and not by sight, regardless of the rising waves that surround me (2 Cor. 5:7).

Lord God, You are my salvation. I will trust in You and not be afraid (Isa. 12:2). *You are in control.*

See also:

1-1. Magnifying the Lord
1-2. Meditating on His Omnipotence and Omnipresence
1-10. Rejoicing in the Face of Discouragement
2-5. Thanking God for the Resurrection of Christ
3-3. Bearing the Fruit of the Spirit
3-9. Building Faith and Trust
5-1. Rest for Sleeplessness
5-8. Courage for Fear
6-4. Financial Difficulties
6-8. Direction for the Future

6

CALMNESS FOR ANGER AND RAGE

So then, my beloved brethren, let every man be swift to hear, slow to speak, slow to wrath; for the wrath of man does not produce the righteousness of God. (James 1:19–20 NKJV)

Almighty God I come before You seething in anger. Only You can bring the raging fire within me under control.

Because I belong to You, I want to be wholly Yours. Please forgive me for giving the devil a foothold—a dwelling place—in my life (Eph. 4:27). Satan, consider this your eviction notice: I rebuke you in the name of Jesus, and I renounce all rights I have given you through my anger. With His own precious blood, I have been purchased by Jesus Christ and I belong to Him (Rev. 5:9).

Dear Jesus, my anger and rage do not produce Your righteousness (James 1:20). Pour Your living water on the fire of my smoldering anger. Quench it completely and fill me with Your love and compassion. Remove the desire for revenge—whether in word or action—because vengeance belongs to You, not me (Rom. 12:19). Since You alone are my judge and advocate, I trust You to come to my defense. I will not be overcome by evil, but I will overcome evil with good (Rom. 12:21).

My heart's desire is to learn how to be angry and yet not sin (Eph. 4:26). Take control of my actions so I can be "swift to hear, slow to speak, slow to wrath" (James 1:19 NKJV). Give me soft answers that will turn away hostility rather than attract it (Prov. 15:1). Free me from justifying my fleshly anger under the appearance of "righteous indignation," and give me the insight to discern the difference between the two.

Heavenly Father, by nature I was a child of wrath—I deserved the full extent of Your judgment (Eph. 2:3). But despite my fatal shortcomings, You forgave me; You raised me up and seated me in the heavenly places so that in the ages to come You might show the exceeding riches of Your grace in Your kindness toward me in Christ Jesus (Eph. 2:5–7). Thank You for showering me with Your grace and mercy. May I respond in kindness, tenderheartedness, and forgiveness the way You have shown me (Eph. 4:31–32).

See also:

1-3. Cherishing God's Love
2-4. Thanking God for His Grace and Mercy
2-6. Thanking God for Making Me the Righteousness of God in Christ
3-2. Growing in Holiness
3-3. Bearing the Fruit of the Spirit
3-9. Building Faith and Trust
4-5. Defeating Gossip and Backbiting
4-11. Letting Go of Bitterness and Unforgiveness
4-12. Victory over Hatred
6-3. Conflict Between Husband and Wife
10-5. Emotional Healing

7

HEALING FOR STRESS-RELATED SICKNESS

> But we have this treasure in earthen vessels, that the excellence of the power may be of God and not of us. We are hard-pressed on every side, yet not crushed; we are perplexed, but not in despair; persecuted, but not forsaken; struck down, but not destroyed—always carrying about in the body the dying of the Lord Jesus, that the life of Jesus also may be manifested in our body. (2 Cor. 4:7–10 NKJV)

Lord Jesus, You didn't design me to shoulder the stress this world offers. Your yoke is easy, and Your burden is light (Matt. 11:30). So I release to You all my pent-up emotions and frustrations: anger, unforgiveness, anxiety, tension, and worry.

I give to you as well any infirmities that may have resulted from carrying the stress you died to free me from: allergies, arthritis, asthma, chronic fatigue, Crohn's Disease, depression, diverticulitis, headaches, high blood pressure, insomnia, irritable bowel syndrome, memory and concentration difficulties, mood swings, myalgic encephalitis, panic attacks, ulcerative colitis, and ulcers. I stand on the promise of Isaiah 53:5 that "by His stripes I am healed" (Isa. 53:5). Cleanse me of the residual affects of stress and tension. May Your life be manifested in my body (2 Cor. 7:10).

Your Word assures me, "The LORD will fight for you, and you shall hold your peace" (Ex. 14:14 NKJV). I repent for responding to stress as if You didn't exist. Because I have sought to fight my own battles and carry the weight of the world on my shoulders, I have lacked the peace only You can give. Please anoint me with the peace that comes from the oil of Your Holy Spirit, and let it flow down to every part of my body. I now free You to fight my battles and carry my burdens.

"You will keep him in perfect peace, / Whose mind is stayed on You, / Because he trusts in You." (Isa. 26:3 NKJV) I resolve to fix my thoughts on Your greatness and Your power. Because You reign over heaven and earth—and over my life—*I will trust in You.*

See also:

1-1. Magnifying the Lord
1-2. Meditating on His Omnipotence and Omnipresence
1-4. Praising God for His Creation
2-3. Thanking God for the Cross and the Blood
2-8. Thanking God for Supplying my Needs
3-9. Building Faith and Trust
4-11. Letting Go of Bitterness and Unforgiveness
4-12. Victory over Hatred
5. Stress
10. Sickness and Disease

8

COURAGE FOR FEAR

Be strong and of good courage, do not fear nor be afraid of them; for the LORD your God, He is the One who goes with you. He will not leave you nor forsake you. (Deut. 31:6 NKJV)

If I were on my own, I would have reason to be afraid. But because You have promised never to leave me nor forsake me, I have nothing to fear (Deut. 31:6).

I thank You, Lord Jesus, that all authority in heaven and on earth has been given to You (Matt. 28:18). All of creation bows down before Your throne (Rev. 5:13), and at the end of the age even the powers of darkness will acknowledge that You are Lord (Phil. 2:10). Because You are greater than any force in heaven, on earth, or under the earth, and You live in me, I will not be overcome by darkness for greater is He who is in me than he who is in the world (1 John 4:4 NASB).

I come against a spirit of fear in the name of the Lord Jesus. God has not given me a spirit of fear, but of power, of love, and of a sound mind (2 Tim. 1:7). Clothe me with Your power from on high (Luke 24:49), fill me with Your perfect love that casts out fear (1 John 4:18), and grant me a Holy Spirit–controlled mind that remains calm in the face of opposition.

Lord God, I place my destiny in Your hands. No weapon formed against me shall prosper, and every tongue that rises against me in judgment I shall condemn. This is *my* heritage as a servant of the Lord (Isa. 54:17).

I will not limit Your power by my own unbelief, but I resolve to walk by faith and not by sight (2 Cor. 5:7). Open my spirit to the battle that rages beyond this mortal existence, and grant me the eyes of faith to live from Your eternal perspective.

I can only walk in one fear: either the fear of God or the fear of man. Inspire me to fear You alone (Jer. 32:40 NIV) because You are the only one I seek approval from.

Instill within me the courage to face giants in the land. When I begin to falter, may my confidence be in the strength of Your right hand and Your promise to be with me wherever I go (Josh. 1:9).

> The LORD is my strength and my song;
>   he has become my salvation.
> Shouts of joy and victory
>   resound in the tents of the righteous:
>   "The LORD's right hand has done mighty things!
>   The LORD's right hand is lifted high;
>   the LORD's right hand has done mighty things!"
> I will not die but live,
>   and will proclaim what the LORD has done.
> (Ps. 118:14–17 NIV)

See also:

1-1. Magnifying the Lord
1-2. Meditating on His Omnipotence and Omnipresence
2-5. Thanking God for the Resurrection of Christ
2-9. Thanking God for His Protection
3-4. Moving in the Gifts of the Spirit
3-9. Building Faith and Trust
11-2. Sharing the Gospel
11-7. Outpouring of Signs and Wonders

9

REDEMPTION IN THE FACE OF TRIBULATION

> For I know that my Redeemer lives,
> And He shall stand at last on the earth;
> And after my skin is destroyed, this I know,
> That in my flesh I shall see God,
> Whom I shall see for myself,
> And my eyes shall behold, and not another.
> How my heart yearns within me! (Job 19:25–27 NKJV)

Despite the storms that rage against me, Lord God, I *will not* become embittered against You. Would that I respond to hardship like Job who refused to doubt Your goodness in the face of relentless tragedy and loss.

For I know that my Redeemer lives. You are *my* Redeemer. You transform the crude sketches in my life into priceless works of art. In Your time, You make all things beautiful (Eccl. 3:11) . . . including my life. Perform Your redemptive work—but give me Your strength to hold on until the end.

My heart's desire is to be more like You. As gold is refined in the fire, purge me of the dross that tarnishes your character in me (Rom. 5:1–4). I look forward to the day when I will be able to see the changes You have made in my life.

You see the big picture—the forest—while I can see only the trees. Although I may not fully understand the reason why I'm in this situation, one thing I do know: You are good and Your mercy endures forever (Ps. 106:1).

Therefore, I will not give up. I will not allow the hardships I face to dictate to me my emotions and responses. Lord, I rest myself in Your care. I trust You. *You are in control, and You know what You're doing.*

See also:

1-1. Magnifying the Lord
1-2. Meditating on His Omnipotence and Omnipresence
1-7. Adoring Christ, the Great "I AM"
1-10. Rejoicing in the Face of Discouragement
2-1. Thanking God for Sending Jesus
2-5. Thanking God for the Resurrection of Christ
2-7. Thanking God for Sending His Spirit
2-8. Thanking God for Supplying my Needs
2-9. Thanking God for His Protection
3-5. Producing Endurance
3-9. Building Faith and Trust
10-9. When God Doesn't Heal

6

MARRIAGE AND FAMILY

You've heard the saying before: The family that prays together, stays together. But why is the family important, and why is prayer such a vital key in keeping it together?

Throughout Scripture, God has used the family unit as the principal means of dealing with His people. Following creation, Adam realized something was missing. Scripture tells us that after surveying and naming every living creature, a suitable helper could not be found (Gen. 2:20b). So God removed a rib from Adam's side and fashioned it into a woman. We then read:

> So God created man in His own image; in the image of God He created him; male and female He created them. *Then God blessed them*, and God said to them, "Be fruitful and multiply; fill the earth and subdue it; have dominion over the fish of the sea, over the birds of the air, and over every living thing that moves on the earth." (Gen. 1:27–28 NKJV, italics added)

Did you notice that God withheld His blessing from Adam

until He gave Eve to be his wife? Since then, God has ordained the family as His primary means of blessing. In the Old Testament, a childless family was deemed to be cursed while a large family was considered blessed (Ps. 127:3–5). Granted, one doesn't have to be married with children in order to be a recipient of God's blessing. Single people and childless couples are equally loved and accepted in God's sight. Yet, every person longs for the safety and nurture only a family can offer.

In some mysterious way, a healthy family points us to a far deeper understanding of the love shared between the Father, Son, and Holy Spirit. God even chose the family—we call ourselves "the family of God"—to describe our membership in the kingdom (Eph. 2:19).

Problems on the home front taint every facet of our lives. A disintegrating marriage undoubtedly affects the child in the classroom and on the playground. Financial stress can make for an irritable coworker. Unfortunately, we can't run away from problems in the home. We expect the world outside to be difficult, but when our safe haven becomes a battle zone, where can we go?

Our family experiences can dramatically affect the way we live our spiritual lives. Growing up with an abusive earthly father can distort our perception of a loving heavenly Father. What we view as normal sibling relationships colors the way we relate to our brothers and sisters in Christ. Family relationships, then, provide the framework by which we work out our salvation, which is why prayer is so important in the family.

The most significant mountains we face arise in the family. Fortunately, God gives us explicit direction in the Bible about what His will is regarding the home so we can approach the throne with confidence. Because we know healthy family relationships are important to God, we can speak to the mountains that stand in the way and see them removed.

1

TO FIND A WIFE

And the LORD God said, "It is not good that man should be alone; I will make him a helper comparable to him." (Gen. 2:18 NKJV)

Lord God, Your Word declares that if I delight myself in You—if I enjoy You and seek Your pleasure above mine—You will give me the desires of my heart (Ps. 37:4). Desiring a wife is not evil or selfish because marriage is honorable (Heb. 13:4). "He who finds a wife finds a good thing, / And obtains favor from the LORD" (Prov. 18:22 NKJV).

At the beginning of creation You proclaimed, "It is not good that man should be alone" (Gen. 2:18 NKJV). You purposely designed me with a void only a wife can fill. So in my divinely created emptiness, I ask You in the name of Jesus to release the wife You have specifically chosen for me.

Because the covenant of marriage is sacred (Mark 10:9), I ask for a woman of God. A woman whose love for me is outmatched only by her love for You. A woman who will inspire me to draw closer to You. A woman who will build me up. A woman whom I can share my deepest thoughts with. A woman whom I will be attracted to physically, emotionally, and spiritually. A woman I will love just as Christ loved the church (Eph. 5:25).

I will not settle for a relationship that is second best, convenient, or one that feeds my insecurities. Guard my purity, and give me the patience to wait. And when I meet her, confirm to me that she is the one.

Free me from any hindrances to a healthy and godly marriage: insecurities, habitual sins, selfishness, emotional hurts, unrealistic expectations. Release from me the baggage of past relationships, and prepare me for the woman You have chosen to be my wife.

In this period of waiting, I will look to You to be my companion and best friend. You are the One who redeems my life from the pit, who crowns me with love and compassion, who satisfies my desires with *good* things (Ps. 103:4–5 NIV). I will not be anxious, but as I present my requests to You, flood me with the peace that surpasses all understanding so my heart and my mind are guarded in Christ Jesus (Phil. 4:6–7).

In this request, I commit myself to trust You and do good, to dwell in the land and feed on Your faithfulness. I commit my way to You and trust that You will bring it to pass (Ps. 37:3–5).

See also:

1-3. Cherishing God's Love
1-7. Adoring Christ, the Great "I AM"
2-8. Thanking God for Supplying My Needs
3-1. Guarding Purity
3-2. Growing in Holiness
3-9. Building Faith and Trust
3-10. Finding Contentment
4-13. Dying to Selfishness
5-2. Peace for Worry
6-12. Single Parents

2

TO FIND A HUSBAND

And the LORD God said, "It is not good that man should be alone; I will make him a helper comparable to him." (Gen. 2:18 NKJV)

Lord God, Your Word declares that if I delight myself in You—if I enjoy You and seek Your pleasure above mine—You will give me the desires of my heart (Ps. 37:4). Desiring a husband is neither evil nor selfish because marriage is honorable (Heb. 13:4).

At the beginning of creation You proclaimed, "It is not good that man should be alone" and then You created Eve to be a suitable partner for Adam (Gen. 2:18). In the name of Jesus, I ask that You would release the husband—a suitable partner—You have chosen for me.

Because the covenant of marriage is sacred (Mark 10:9), I ask for a man of God. Please give me a husband whose love for me is outmatched only by His love for You. A man who will cherish me and build me up (Prov. 31:28). A man who will honor me (1 Peter 3:7) and our marriage vows. A man who is a good father and provider. A man whom I will be attracted to physically, emotionally, and spiritually. A man who will love me as Christ loved the church (Eph. 5:25).

Restrain me from attaching myself to another man out of desperation. I will not settle for a relationship that is second best, convenient, or one that feeds my insecurities. Guard my purity, and give me the patience to wait. And when I meet him, confirm to me that he is the one.

Release from me the baggage of past relationships, and prepare me for the man You have chosen to be my husband. Free me from any hindrances to a healthy and godly marriage: insecurities, habitual sins, selfishness, emotional hurts. Dispel my unrealistic expectations that set me up for disappointment. I place my trust in You rather than my partner.

In this period of waiting I will look to You to be my companion and best friend. You are the One who redeems my life from the pit, who crowns me with love and compassion, who satisfies my desires with *good* things (Ps. 103:4–5 NIV). I will not be anxious, but as I present my requests to You, flood me with the peace that surpasses all understanding so my heart and my mind are guarded in Christ Jesus (Phil. 4:6–7).

In this request, I commit myself to trust You and do good, to dwell in the land and feed on Your faithfulness. I commit my way to You and trust that You will bring it to pass (Ps. 37:3–5).

See also:

1-3. Cherishing God's Love
1-7. Adoring Christ, the Great "I AM"
2-6. Thanking God for Making Me the Righteousness of God in Christ
2-8. Thanking God for Supplying my Needs
3-1. Guarding Purity
3-2. Growing in Holiness
3-10. Finding Contentment
4-13. Dying to Selfishness
5-2. Peace for Worry
6-12. Single Parents

3

CONFLICT BETWEEN HUSBAND AND WIFE

> But the wisdom that is from above is first pure, then peaceable, gentle, *willing to yield*, full of mercy and good fruits, without partiality and without hypocrisy. Now the fruit of righteousness is sown in peace by those who make peace. (James 3:17–18 NKJV, italics added)

Lord God, Your Word proclaims that all things work together for good to those who love You (Rom. 8:28). In the midst of my marital crossfire, I trust that You are working something good.

Regardless how our conflict began, I bless my spouse (Matt. 5:44). Overwhelm me with Your love and compassion. I will not allow dissension to drive a wedge between the two of us. Therefore what You have joined together, let neither my spouse nor I separate (Matt. 19:6).

More than changing my spouse, Lord, change me. I want to be more like You. May You increase and I decrease (John 3:30). Search my heart and weed out any pride that prevents me from being part of the solution rather than the problem. I can't be so arrogant as to assume I have no liability in our disagreement. Convict me of my sin. Cultivate Your humility in me so I can openly confess my wrongdoing and be restored.

What part my spouse is responsible for in our conflict, change her (or him). No matter how hard I try, no matter how well I can argue, I am incapable of changing my spouse, so I release her (or him) to the conviction of Your Holy Spirit. I refuse to usurp Your role in my spouse's life.

I lay aside all anger, wrath, resentment, and offenses of the past. My love keeps no record of wrongs but always protects, always trusts, always hopes, always perseveres (1 Cor. 13:5b,7 NIV). It's to my glory to overlook an offense (Prov. 19:11 NIV) so I forgive my spouse for any hurts that have been inflicted—whether accidental or intentional. I will not be ensnared by the devil through foolish and ignorant disputes (2 Tim 2:23).

I place a hedge of protection around my household (Job 1:10) that the enemy would not have a foothold in the covenant my spouse and I have established with God (Eph. 4:26–27). Show us that we are on the same side fighting one opponent.

The wisdom that comes from above is willing to yield (James 3:17). Grant me Your wisdom to discern my fleshly desires from truth. Give me a sense of which battles are worth fighting and which ones aren't.

More importantly, restore us so we can live together again in agreement. Strengthen us as a result of our conflict, and draw us closer to one another. May the seeds of peace sown in our relationship yield a harvest of righteousness (James 3:18).

See also:

1-8. Worshiping in Spirit and Truth
1-10. Rejoicing in the Face of Discouragement
2-3. Thanking God for the Cross and the Blood
2-4. Thanking God for His Grace and Mercy
3-3. Bearing the Fruit of the Spirit
4-3. Overcoming Pride
4-11. Letting Go of Bitterness and Unforgiveness
5-6. Calmness for Anger and Rage

4

FINANCIAL DIFFICULTIES

And God is able to make all grace abound toward you, that you, always having all sufficiency in all things, may have an abundance for every good work. (2 Cor 9:8 NIV)

Though You were rich, Lord Jesus, yet for my sake You became poor, so that through Your poverty I might become rich (2 Cor. 8:9). I rejoice in knowing that You have spared no expense in sharing the riches of heaven with me: My sins are forgiven (Eph. 1:7), I have the gift of eternal life (John 3:16), and I am seated in the heavenly places in Christ Jesus (Eph. 2:6).

In agreement with Your Word, I ask that You would supply all my financial needs according to Your riches in glory by Christ Jesus (Phil. 4:19). You are able to make all grace abound toward me, that I, always having all sufficiency in all things, may have an abundance for every good work (2 Cor. 9:8).

Lord, You withhold no good thing from those who walk uprightly (Ps. 84:11). Reveal to me any thoughts or actions that hinder the flow of Your blessing. If I am living in disobedience, turn me around and bring me to repentance (Deut. 30:16). If I have strayed from Your will, direct me back to Your path (Prov. 3:6). If I lack the confidence to step out, increase my faith (Mark 9:24).

Godliness with contentment is great gain (1 Tim. 6:6). Cleanse me of any greed, selfishness, or materialism that seeks to hoard Your blessings rather than share them (2 Cor. 9:11 NIV). I want to be a channel of Your blessing, not merely a recipient (Gen. 12:2–3).

Bring to light any areas where I may be robbing You by withholding what rightfully belongs to You. When I bring the whole tithe into the storehouse, You challenge me to test You and see if You will not throw open the floodgates of heaven and pour out so much blessing that I will not have enough room for it (Mal. 3:8–10 NIV). Therefore, I will not withhold anything from You.

Satan, you are a thief, and you come only to kill, steal, and destroy (John 10:10). According to Matt. 18:18, whatever I bind on earth will be bound in heaven and whatever I loose on earth will be loosed in heaven. So in the name Jesus, I bind you from stealing from me, and I command you to return what you have stolen. Financial roadblocks, I strike you down, and by the grace of Jesus Christ I loose His abundant life (John 10:10).

I place my trust, dear God, in Your goodness. When I ask for bread, You will not give me a stone. When I ask for a fish, You will not give me a serpent. If I, in my sin-laden condition, know how to give good gifts, how much more will You give good gifts to those who ask You (Matt. 7:9–11)? So hear my request, and by Your grace lead me out of my financial straits and into Your promised land of provision and abundance.

See also:

1-1. Magnifying the Lord
1-2. Meditating on His Omnipotence and Omnipresence
2-8. Thanking God for Supplying my Needs
3-9. Building Faith and Trust
3-10. Finding Contentment
4-6. Triumphing over Greed, Indulgence, and Materialism
4-8. Winning over Laziness
4-13. Dying to Selfishness
9-6. Favor

5

CHILDLESSNESS

Now Isaac pleaded with the LORD for his wife, because she was barren; and the LORD granted his plea, and Rebekah his wife conceived. (Gen. 25:21 NKJV)

So great was Your love, heavenly Father, that You created man and woman—Your own offspring—to share in it. Thank You for pouring out Your love on me and accepting me as a child of God (John 1:12). And since our inception, You have placed deep within us the desire to share our love with our offspring, too. The yearning to "be fruitful and multiply" (Gen. 1:22) is neither sinful nor selfish, because the desire comes from You.

In my pain and frustration I ask for a child I can pour out my love upon as well. "Behold, children are a heritage from the LORD, / The fruit of the womb is His reward" (Ps. 127:3 NKJV). Grant my spouse and me our godly heritage, and give to us the fruit of the womb. Like Jacob, I refuse to let go of You until I receive a blessing, a child whom I can call my own (Gen. 32:26).

Replace my anger and frustration with the peace that surpasses all understanding (Phil. 4:7). Transform my discouragement into a hope that refuses to give up. Heal the pain that results from endless disappointments. You are my peace (Isa. 9:6). You are my living hope (1 Peter 1:3). And You are my healer (Ex. 15:26).

I speak the atoning blood of Jesus over my spouse and me. By His stripes we are healed (Isa. 53:5): body, soul, and spirit. Just as Isaac pleaded with You for his wife, and Rebekah conceived, so I plead with You to bring healing to our bodies so we can conceive (Gen. 25:21).

Nurture in me a sense of esteem that is independent of our ability to procreate. My identity doesn't come from the children I have, but from whose child I am.

Thank You that He who began a good work in me will continue it until the day of Christ Jesus (Phil 1:6). I place my trust in the good work You are accomplishing in my life. I seek Your kingdom and Your righteousness knowing that all these things will be added unto me (Matt. 6:33). I speak these things in the life-giving name of Jesus Christ.

See also:

1-3. Cherishing God's Love
1-4. Praising God for His Creation
1-10. Rejoicing in the Face of Discouragement
2-6. Thanking God for Making Me the Righteousness of God in Christ
3-5. Producing Endurance
3-9. Building Faith and Trust
5-3. Hope for Despair
5-6. Calmness for Anger and Rage

6

TIME STRUGGLES

See then that you walk circumspectly, not as fools but as wise, redeeming the time, because the days are evil. (Eph. 5:15–16 NKJV)

Almighty God, pulled in every direction by the concerns of this world I feel as if my life is at a stalemate. The infinite demands of work, church, and other obligations compete for time in a finite schedule. I confess that in the end, my relationships with family and with You suffer the greatest.

Yet the words of Your son Jesus bring me back to what really matters, "For what is a man profited if he gains the whole world, and loses his own soul? Or what will a man give in exchange for his soul?" (Matt. 16:26 NKJV). With earnest conviction I confess, *I will not forfeit my relationship with You nor my family in order to gain this world's approval.*

I commit myself to spending quality, quantity time with You. Nothing is more important than investing in our relationship. You did not give me a spirit of timidity, but a spirit of power, of love, and of *self-discipline* (2 Tim. 1:7 NIV, italics added). Work Your discipline in me so I will consciously set aside the time to grow deeper in maturity. Open up the riches of Your Word and meet me in prayer so my heart will work in conjunction with my intentions.

I commit myself to spending quality, quantity time with my family. Give me the discernment and foresight to say no to the urgent and yes to the important. Show me *Your* priorities and impart to me the measure of faith to put them into practice. I want to live up to Your expectations of a spouse and parent.

Please multiply back to me the seeds I have sown that I would reap a harvest of righteousness, effectiveness, and, ultimately, thanksgiving to God.

> Now may He who supplies seed to the sower, and bread for food, supply and multiply the seed you have sown and increase the fruits of your righteousness, while you are enriched in everything for all liberality, which causes thanksgiving through us to God. (2 Cor. 9:10–11 NKJV)

See also:

1-2. Meditating on His Omnipotence and Omnipresence
1-4. Praising God for His creation
1-9. Loving God's Will
2-8. Thanking God for Supplying my Needs
3-8. Joining God in His Will
3-10. Finding Contentment

7

PHYSICAL OR EMOTIONAL ABUSE

Let the husband render to his wife the affection due her, and likewise also the wife to her husband. (1 Cor. 7:3 NKJV)

Heavenly Father, I come to You a broken person. The physical and emotional scars of an abusive spouse have battered me to the point of despondency. I desperately need Your presence and power.

Please dispatch Your angels as a hedge of protection around my family (Job 1:10). Shield us from further harm. "For You, O LORD, will bless the righteous; / With favor You will surround him as with a shield" (Ps. 5:12 NKJV).

I bind the spirit of anger, vengeance, and violence over my spouse and my family. Satan, in the name of Jesus I forbid you from gaining a foothold into our lives through this abuse. You are a thief, and you come only to steal, kill, and destroy, but Jesus came that our family would manifest His abundant life (John 10:10).

I loose peace, calmness, and self-control into my spouse. May he (or she) love me not only in word or in tongue, but in deed and in truth (1 John 3:18). Transplant from within my spouse a heart of stone into a heart of flesh (Ezek. 36:26).

In the name of Jesus, I come against a spirit of condemnation over my family. "There is therefore now no condemnation to those who are in Christ Jesus" (Rom. 8:1 NKJV). Disperse the enemy's smoke screen that tells me our problem is my fault. Because I am in Christ Jesus I refuse to bear the blame for the behavior of others, nor do I allow it to take root in my family. Lord Jesus, put a stop to this generational sin and prevent us from acting out what we have experienced.

God, as a member of the covenantal relationship with my spouse, I earnestly plead for Your divine intervention. Do whatever it takes to bring repentance to my spouse and restoration to our marriage (Ezek. 33:11).

"You are my hiding place; / You shall preserve me from trouble; / You shall surround me with songs of deliverance" (Ps. 32:7 NKJV). Sing to me Your precious songs of deliverance. Remove the venomous arrows that have pierced my damaged soul and heal me with Your atoning blood (Isa. 53:5).

In this time of confusion, instill within me the strength to continue (Eph. 6:13), the courage to confide in someone who can help me (Prov. 15:22), and the wisdom to know where to go from here.

Thank You for bestowing upon me beauty for ashes, the oil of joy for mourning, and the garment of praise for heaviness. May I be called a tree of righteousness, the planting of the Lord, that You may be glorified (Isa. 61:3).

See also:

1-3. Cherishing God's Love
1-4. Praising God for His Creation
1-10. Rejoicing in the face of Discouragement
2-9. Thanking God for His Protection
4-11. Letting Go of Bitterness and Unforgiveness
4-12. Victory over Hatred
5-6. Calmness for Anger and Rage
5-8. Courage for Fear

8

DIRECTION FOR THE FUTURE

For this reason we also, since the day we heard it, do not cease to pray for you, and to ask that you may be filled with the knowledge of His will in all wisdom and spiritual understanding; that you may walk worthy of the Lord, fully pleasing Him, being fruitful in every good work and increasing in the knowledge of God. (Col. 1:9–10 NKJV)

God of all wisdom, I come before You seeking Your guidance. My earnest desire is to do Your will; may Your kingdom come and Your will be done in my life as it is in heaven (Matt. 6:10).

Cleanse me of any worldly wisdom or selfish motives—the lust of the flesh, the lust of the eyes, and the pride of life—that draw me away from Your purposes (1 John 2:15-17). May You count me worthy of Your calling, and by Your power may You fulfill every good purpose and every act prompted by my faith (2 Thess. 1:11 NIV).

I refuse to respond according to my own wisdom and strength. In accordance with James 1:5–8, I ask for *Your* wisdom regarding my future, knowing that You give to everyone liberally and without reproach. I ask in faith—without doubting—expecting Your divine direction. In advance I thank You for the wisdom You assure me You will give.

Oh, the depth of the riches both of Your wisdom and knowledge! How unsearchable are Your judgments and unfathomable Your ways (Rom. 11:33 NASB)!

Give me the courage to follow the pathway of faith, not fear, for You have not given me a spirit of fear, but of power and of love and of a sound mind (2 Tim. 1:7). Endue me with Your power (Luke 24:49), clothe me in Your love that casts out all fear (1 John 4:18), and guide me with the mind of Christ (1 Cor. 2:16). I resolve to walk by faith and not by sight (2 Cor. 5:7).

Strengthen me to take the path You have set before me and not the path of least resistance, because narrow is the gate and difficult is the way that leads to life, and there are few who find it (Matt. 7:14).

Therefore, reveal to me Your clear direction. Speak to me that You would work in me both to will and to do Your good pleasure (Phil. 2:13).

See also:

1-2. Meditating on His Omnipotence and Omnipresence
1-5. Acclaiming God's Majesty and the Beauty of Holiness
1-9. Loving God's Will
2-2. Thanking God for His Word
2-8. Thanking God for Supplying my Needs
3-6. Learning Obedience
3-8. Joining God in His Will
3-9. Building Faith and Trust
4-9. Giving God Control of Selfish Ambition
5-2. Peace for Worry
5-8. Courage for Fear
9-1. Wisdom and Guidance in Your Job Search
9-7. Purpose in the Workplace

9

UNSAVED SPOUSE

> And he brought them out and said, "Sirs, what must I do to be saved?" So they said, "Believe on the Lord Jesus Christ, and you will be saved, you and your household." (Acts 16:30–31 NKJV)

Heavenly Father, because of Your great mercy You are not willing that any should perish but that all should come to repentance (2 Peter 3:9). I know that when I bring this request before You, I am in alignment with Your will because You desire all men to be saved and to come to the knowledge of the truth (1 Tim. 2:4).

So I come before Your throne with boldness, standing on Your Word:

> Now this is the confidence that we have in Him, that if we ask anything according to His will, He hears us. And if we know that He hears us, whatever we ask, we know that we have the petitions that we have asked of Him. (1 John 5:14–15)

Lord Jesus, You love my spouse more than I do, and when You were hanging on that cross You were thinking not only of me, but him (or her) as well. In the name of Jesus I bind the powers of darkness from deceiving my spouse from the truth. Close his (or her) eyes to deception (1 John 1:8). Shut his (or her) ears from the lies of the enemy (John 8:44 NIV). Remove any influences that would draw him (or her) away from You. In its place I loose the spirit of adoption (Rom. 8:15). Like a hound hot on the trail of its prey, O Hound of Heaven, doggedly pursue my spouse. I release You to do whatever it takes to bring my spouse to the place of complete submission to Your Lordship.

There is nothing I can do to change his (or her) heart. But You can. Open his (or her) eyes to the truth of Your Word (Ps. 119:18). Take his (or her) heart of stone and transform it into a heart of flesh (Ezek. 36:26). Draw people into my spouse's path who would point him(or her) to Jesus Christ and share the words of eternal life.

As a believing member of our one-flesh covenant, my unbelieving spouse is sanctified—set apart and made holy (1 Cor 7:14). Bring him (or her) under the conviction of Your Holy Spirit (John 16:8) so our unequal yoke can be replaced with an equal yoke (2 Cor. 6:14).

Show me my role in Your redemptive plan for my spouse. Set a guard over my mouth (Ps. 141:3) and guide my actions so I won't hinder Your Spirit's work.

On this day I make this proclamation: But as for me and my house, *we* will serve the LORD (Josh. 24:15).

See also:

1-6. Yearning for More of Jesus
1-9. Loving God's Will
1-10. Rejoicing in the Face of Discouragement
2-1. Thanking God for Sending Jesus
2-3. Thanking God for the Cross and the Blood
2-4. Thanking God for His Grace and Mercy
2-10. Thanking God for Choosing Me
3-8. Joining God in His Will
4-1. The Prayer of Salvation (Sinner's Prayer)
7-4. For the Salvation of Your Child
11. Bringing in the Kingdom of God

10

MOVING

Be strong and of good courage, do not fear nor be afraid of them; for the LORD your God, He is the One who goes with you. He will not leave you nor forsake you. (Deut. 31:6 NKJV)

Redeeming Father, the winds of change have led me into the unknown. Without Your presence going before me, I would be afraid, but because You promise to be with me always, I have no reason to fear (Deut. 31:6).

My faith rests not in my ever-changing circumstances but in Jesus, the same yesterday, today, and forever (Heb. 13:8). Day in and day out, Your faithfulness and goodness never change.

I find comfort in knowing that Your plans for my life include prosperity, safety, hope, and a future (Jer. 29:11 NIV). "The path of the righteous is like the first gleam of dawn, / shining ever brighter till the full light of day" (Prov. 4:18 NIV).

Like forgiveness, moving to new surroundings presents the opportunity start over (2 Cor. 5:17). In this move I leave behind the negative habits of the past and add to my faith goodness, knowledge, self-control, perseverance, godliness, brotherly kindness, and love in increasing measure. May I grow effective and productive in my knowledge of You in this new adventure (2 Peter 1:5–8).

Spur new relationships with our family members that would provoke us toward love and good works (Heb. 10:24). Lead us to a congregation of Your people that would challenge us to grow deeper in our walk with You and inspire us to live our faith. Draw us into redemptive relationships that would create opportunities to boldly share the good news of salvation in an atmosphere of safety and trust (Rom. 1:16).

By Your Holy Spirit, make this adjustment easy for our children. Please bring friends into their lives who are respectful and godly. Use this situation to make them increasingly reliant upon You.

Jesus, I trust that You are the Good Shepherd (John 10:11) and that You have led us here to green pastures and still waters (Ps. 23:2). Please send me reminders along the way of Your grace to confirm that You have brought us here.

See also:

1-7. Adoring Christ, the Great "I AM"
1-9. Loving God's Will
2-7. Thanking God for Sending His Spirit
2-8. Thanking God for Supplying my Needs
3-9. Building Faith and Trust
5-4. Order for Confusion
5-8. Courage for Fear
6-8. Direction for the Future

11

WORKING PARENTS

He gives power to the weak,
And to those who have no might He increases strength.
Even the youths shall faint and be weary,
And the young men shall utterly fall,
But those who wait on the LORD
Shall renew their strength;
They shall mount up with wings like eagles,
They shall run and not be weary,
They shall walk and not faint. (Isa. 40:29–31 NKJV)

Father God, I need Your understanding and empowerment to sort through my dilemma.

Juggling the responsibilities of a provider and parent is precarious: On the one hand if I don't provide for my family, I have denied the faith and I am worse than an unbeliever (1 Tim. 5:8). On the other hand, if I neglect my parental responsibility, I have squandered the role You have given me of raising my children up in the training and admonition of You (Eph. 6:4). By Your grace, grant me the insight to know how to navigate between the two.

Reawaken within me a sense of what is important. Knowing You, loving You, and becoming more like You is my highest calling (Phil. 1:9–11). Draw me back to You when I allow our relationship to take secondary importance. And when we're together, make our time fruitful.

Fostering an ever-deepening relationship with my spouse is so easy to overlook. Give us creative ideas that enable us to enjoy one another apart from the rest of the family. Nurture between us an intimacy that flourishes just as it did when we were first married (Prov. 5:18).

The stress of working and being a good parent is formidable. Give me the wisdom to train up my child (or children) in the way he should go, so that when he is old he will not depart from it (Prov. 22:6). In those moments when I lack the energy to parent effectively, infuse me with Your strength (Isa. 40:29–31). May Your strength be made perfect in my weakness (2 Cor. 12:9).

Nothing can replace the time I spend with my family. Convict me when I sacrifice family relationships at the altar of materialism and greed—all in the name of "a better lifestyle" (Luke 12:13–21). Bless us financially enough so I don't have to work excessively in order to make ends meet and give me a sense of when enough is enough.

Free me from the bondage of having to be the perfect Christian, the perfect marriage partner, and the perfect parent. I want to be the Christian, spouse, and parent You have called me to be, but You are the only One who is perfect (Deut. 32:4). Thank You for Your all-sufficient grace that fills in the gaps where I come up short (2 Cor. 12:9).

See also:

1-6. Yearning for More of Jesus
1-8. Worshiping in Spirit and Truth
2-8. Thanking God for Supplying my Needs
3-10. Finding Contentment
5. Stress
6. Marriage and Family
7. The Lives of Your Children
9. Job and Career

12

SINGLE PARENTS

What then shall we say to these things? If God is for us, who can *be* against us? He who did not spare His own Son, but delivered Him up for us all, how shall He not with Him also freely give us all things? (Rom. 8:31–32 NKJV)

Almighty God, my greatest consolation is knowing that You are just. A father to the fatherless, a defender of widows, You are my holy habitation (Ps. 68:5). You understand the dilemmas I face and You work on my behalf as I wait on You. "For since the world began, no ear has heard, and no eye has seen a God like you, who works for those who wait for him!" (Isa. 64:4 NLT).

Lord Jesus, You are the great "I AM" and everything I will ever need: You're my provider (Phil. 4:19), my spouse (2 Cor. 11:2), my best friend (John 15:13–15), my constant companion (Deut. 31:6), my adviser (Prov. 2:6–7) . . . and You exceed my greatest expectations (Eph. 3:20–21). Fill in the gaps that inevitably arise from being a single parent.

You are the Alpha and the Omega, the Beginning and the End (Rev. 1:8), the God who reigns over time. Multiply my limited time so I can accomplish the limitless tasks required of single parenthood.

You give power to the weak, and to those who *have* no might You increase strength. (Isa. 40:29). Strengthen me to work with diligence at my job, come home, and still have enough energy to raise my child (or children).

Supporting a family on a single income forces me to rely on You. I depend upon the trustworthiness of Your word that You will to supply all our needs according to Your riches in glory by Christ Jesus (Phil. 4:19). Father God, because You didn't spare Your own Son on my behalf, I trust You to provide us with everything we need (Rom. 8:31–32).

Living without a spouse, I need the parenting skills to function as both mother *and* father. Show me how to balance the roles of nurturer and disciplinarian. Give me Your wisdom to train up my child (or children) in the way he (or she) should go, so that when he (or she) is old he (or she) will not depart from it (Prov. 22:6). Investing myself into the life of my child (or children) is my highest calling.

In those times when I am lonely or feeling sorry for myself, fill me with the glory of Your presence (Isa. 6). Reassure me that You are at my side, guiding me every step of the way.

See also:

1-3. Cherishing God's Love
1-6. Yearning for More of Jesus
1-7. Adoring Christ, the Great "I AM"
2-6. Thanking God for Making Me the Righteousness of God in Christ
2-8. Thanking God for Supplying my Needs
3-5. Producing Endurance
3-9. Building Faith and Trust
6-1. To Find a Wife
6-2. To Find a Husband
6-4. Financial Difficulties
6-6. Time Struggles
6-11. Working Parents
7. The Lives of Your Children

13

SEPARATION AND DIVORCE

Always in every prayer of mine, I make requests for you all with joy, for your fellowship in the gospel from the first day until now, being confident of this very thing, that He who has begun a good work un you will complete it until the day of Jesus Christ. (Phil. 1:4–6)

Father God, it's no wonder You declare in Your Word, "I hate divorce" (Mal. 2:16 NKJV). The pain of tearing apart my divinely-sealed covenant is far greater than You ever intended me to bear. I confess my sin and take responsibility for my part in our downfall (Matt. 19:6). Please forgive me and cleanse me of the residual effects of my divorce (1 John 1:9).

Even when I walk through the valley of the shadow of death, I know You are with me (Ps. 23:4). Weeping when I weep. Encouraging me when I feel discouraged. Giving me hope to go on. Thank You for never giving up on me.

By Your grace, mend my broken heart and comfort me in my grief. Give me beauty for ashes, the oil of joy for mourning, and the garment of praise for heaviness. May this be the acceptable year of the Lord.

Use this tragedy in my life as an opportunity for growth. Soften my rough edges that hinder true intimacy. Water the seeds of my brokenness that I would bear an ever-increasing harvest of the fruit of the Spirit (Gal. 5:22–23).

Rebuild the remnants of my shattered soul. Re-establish my

identity not on what I have done or what has been done to me, but on what Christ has done *for* me. Thank You for transforming me into the righteousness of God in Christ (2 Cor. 5:21).

I refuse to carry the yoke of unforgiveness and bitterness toward my estranged spouse. Your yoke is easy, and Your burden is light (Matt. 11:30). Despite the hurt and pain I have suffered, what You endured on the cross for my sins was far greater. Yet You forgave me (1 Peter 3:18). So I release every burden and bondage into Your hands.

Guard me from rushing into relationships that seek to fill the emptiness only You can supply. My fulfillment can only be found in You (Ps. 107:9).

Thank you that divorce is not the unpardonable sin. Use the hurts of my past to bring healing and wholeness *to* me and ultimately *through* me into the lives of others that I may be called a tree of righteousness. And that You may be glorified (Isa. 61:3).

See also:

1-3. Cherishing God's Love
1-10. Rejoicing in the Face of Discouragement
2-6. Thanking God for Making Me the Righteousness of God in Christ
2-10. Thanking God for Choosing Me
3-10. Finding Contentment
4-11. Letting Go of Bitterness and Unforgiveness
4-12. Victory over Hatred
5-3. Hope for Despair
5-6. Calmness for Anger and Rage
6-12. Single Parents

7

THE LIVES OF YOUR CHILDREN

Perhaps the greatest ministry parents can undertake is to pray for their children.

All too often we busy ourselves to such a great extent—even doing the Lord's business—that we fail to minister to those whom God has specifically called us *to*. We may be a success on the business front or the ministry front, but if we neglect to train up our children in the way they should go—in the training and admonition of the Lord (Eph. 6:4)—we have fallen miserably short. To put a twist on a familiar Scripture: "For what will it profit a man if he gains the whole world, and loses his own family?" (Mark 8:36).

Into the hands of each parent, God has placed the responsibility of raising a child not only to be a responsible, productive adult, but a *godly* man or woman as well. Our actions in the lives of our children pay dividends throughout the rest of their lives: If we sow seeds of negativity or harm, we will ultimately reap a harvest of negativity and further harm. If not toward us, then toward others. If we sow seeds of righteousness and love, we will ultimately reap a harvest of further righteousness and love.

At the same time, releasing a child into the perils of a world that is no longer safe can leave a parent feeling powerless. What happens if someone abuses your son? What if your daughter gets a teacher who humiliates her in front of the class? What if your child starts hanging around the wrong crowd? There are so many variables that lie beyond our control. But as much as we would like, governing every area of their life is not only untenable, it's downright unhealthy. And yet there is something remotely healthy about entrusting them to God.

The one variable we *can* control is the decision to pray for our children. No one knows our children like we do. No one can pray as specifically (and therefore as effectively) as we do. No one cares for our children like we do. Our prayer waters the seeds of righteousness and love we sow into their lives.

Praying for our children is not enough. But prayer coupled with godly parenting gives our children a chance to see the mountains in their lives moved.

1

FOR YOUR UNBORN CHILD

> Then the word of the LORD came to me, saying:
> "Before I formed you in the womb I knew you;
> Before you were born I sanctified you;
> And I ordained you a prophet to the nations."
> (Jer. 1:4–5 NKJV)

Lord Jesus, Your Word decrees that You already know the child inside my womb, that you love him (or her), and that You've ordained this baby for a special purpose. I am overwhelmed with the knowledge that You know everything about my child's life and future: hopes, dreams, successes, failures, beginning . . . and end (Acts 17:26).

Like Abraham, I withhold nothing—not even my child—from You (Gen. 22:9–19). Therefore, I offer him (or her) to You on the altar of my own hopes and dreams, and I am comforted by the knowledge that this child is in *Your* hands—not mine—now and forever.

Lord, please bless my child with health. Your Word declares, "Out of the mouth of babes and nursing infants / You have ordained strength" (Ps. 8:2 NKJV). Strengthen my child according to Your Word. In the name of Jesus, I rebuke the spirit of physical infirmity and forbid it from prevailing over my child and me (Luke 13:11–12). I pray that no evil shall befall my child, nor any plague come near the dwelling of my womb (Ps. 91:10). May Your presence in me be increased, even now, so nothing evil will touch my baby or my body except that which comes from You.

Sanctify—set apart for Your purposes—my child, just as You sanctified Jeremiah. Appoint him (or her) over nations and kingdoms to uproot and tear down, to destroy and overthrow, to build and to plant (Jer. 1:10). May he (or she) live to glorify Your name and, above all, may he (or she) grow to know You, just as You know him (or she) (John 17:25), despite the trials and tribulations he (or she) will inevitably face.

"Every good and perfect gift is from above" (James 1:17). Thank You, Lord, for giving me this good and perfect gift. I praise You for this blessing of new life.

See also:

1-4. Praising God for His Creation
1-5. Acclaiming God's Majesty and the Beauty of Holiness
2-1. Thanking God for Sending Jesus
2-7. Thanking God for Sending His Spirit
2-9. Thanking God for His Protection
3-9. Building Faith and Trust
5-2. Peace for Worry
10-6. Protection from Sickness and Disease

2

WHEN YOU ARE IN CONFLICT WITH YOUR CHILD

And he arose and came to his father. But when he was still a great way off, his father saw him and had compassion, and ran and fell on his neck and kissed him. (Luke 15:20 NKJV)

Holy Spirit, comfort me now, because I desire to hold my child like the father held the prodigal son. But, there are no hugs or kisses—only enmity and distrust. I'm distressed, Lord, to have the knowledge of Your love and peace, but to not live in it.

Father God, You said in Your Word that You will turn the hearts of the fathers to the children and the hearts of the children to their fathers (Mal. 4:6). I plead with You to turn our hearts toward each other. Grant us the ability to not only forgive, but be reconciled. Meld our hearts in one accord by Your Spirit, forgetting each other's shortcomings.

If I have sinned against my child and provoked him (or her) to discouragement (Col. 3:21), I plead for Your forgiveness. Give me the courage to admit my fault to my child and be restored. May my speech be with grace, seasoned with salt, that I may know how to make things right with my child (1 John 4:6).

If my child has sinned against me, give me the grace to forgive. I forsake my stubborn attitudes and leave the responsibility of judging him (or her) with You (Matt 7:1). By Your power I turn the other cheek toward my child (Luke 6:29). In the name of Jesus, I rebuke the obstinate spirit that's taken root in our relationship, and thank You in advance for breaking down the walls that divide us.

I know that everything works together for good, so my hope for peace with my child rests confidently in You (Ps. 39:7). You are the Prince of Peace, and I accept Your peaceful ways to bring a harmonious end to the strife that separates us. Your Word says two are better than one because if one of us falls, the other can help him up. Help us, Lord, then to pick one other up instead of pushing each other down (Eccl. 4:9–12).

See also:

1-3. Cherishing God's Love
1-10. Rejoicing in the Face of Discouragement
2-3. Thanking God for the Cross and the Blood
2-4. Thanking God for His Grace and Mercy
3-2. Growing in Holiness
4-11. Letting Go of Bitterness and Unforgiveness
4-12. Victory over Hatred
5-6. Calmness for Anger and Rage

3

WHEN YOUR CHILD IS REBELLIOUS

To him the doorkeeper opens, and the sheep hear his voice; and he calls his own sheep by name and leads them out. And when he brings out his own sheep, he goes before them; and the sheep follow him, for they know his voice. Yet they will by no means follow a stranger, but will flee from him, for they do not know the voice of strangers. (John 10:3–5 NKJV)

Father God, You, above all, understand the aching in my heart. You promise in Your Word that if I train up my child in Your ways, when he (or she) is older he will not depart from it (Prov. 22:6). I have made my ways Your ways, Lord, and I've taught my child to do the same.

But now, Lord, the enemy has come between my child and You. There are rebellious attitudes, defiance, and disobedience to Your ways. I realize that according to Your Word, rebellion is as the sin of witchcraft, and stubbornness is as idolatry (1 Sam. 15:23). You rejected Saul from his place of privilege because of his rebellion, and I am concerned that You may reject my child for the same reason (1 Sam. 13:13–14).

So, by the power of the name of Jesus, I take authority over the spirit of witchcraft in the life of my child. Satan, you have no right to establish residence in my child's life. Be gone in the name of Jesus!

Jesus, purify and make holy the heart of my child. May he (or she) seek first Your kingdom and Your righteousness (Matt. 6:33), fulfilling Your purposes, and not his (or her) own purposes or the enemy's.

Lord Jesus, You're the good shepherd, and You gave Your life to bring the stray sheep back into the fold. Like You, I desire to do whatever it takes to bring my child—Your prodigal sheep—back into Your fold. Please grant me Your wisdom to know how (John 10:11–18).

Forgive me, Jesus, for allowing worry and anxiety to overwhelm me regarding my child's rebellious ways. Your yoke is easy, and Your burden is light (Matt. 11:30). Therefore, I give You this weight bearing down on my shoulders. Because You are slow to anger and abounding in mercy (Ps. 103:8), I trust that You will preserve my child in spite of his (or her) rebellion, and that in due season, Your presence will increase in his (or her) life.

Bring back to my child's remembrance the loving sound of Your voice. As You call out his (or her) name, may he (or she) follow You, the Good Shepherd, back into Your fold.

See also:

1-8. Worshiping in Spirit and Truth
1-9. Loving God's Will
2-4. Thanking God for His Grace and Mercy
2-10. Thanking God for Choosing Me
3-6. Learning Obedience
3-8. Joining God in His Will
3-9. Building Faith and Trust
4-13. Dying to Selfishness
4-15. Finding Freedom from Rebellion
5-2. Peace for Worry
5-8. Courage for Fear

4

FOR THE SALVATION OF YOUR CHILD

And Jesus said to [Zacchaeus], "Today salvation has come to this house . . . for the Son of Man has come to seek and to save that which was lost." (Luke 19:9–10 NKJV)

Heavenly Father, as much as I love my child, I know You love him (or her) more.

I come to You and intercede on behalf of my unsaved child. Please visit our home just as You did Zacchaeus's. With great anticipation and faith I speak to my family, "Today salvation has come to this house" (Luke 19:9)! We need a visitation from You!

Your Word says, "Believe on the Lord Jesus Christ, and you will be saved, you *and your household*" (Acts 16:31 NKJV, italics added). Because I have believed on the Lord Jesus Christ, I am confident that through the work of the Holy Spirit, my child will soon believe as well.

I speak the spirit of adoption over my child (Rom. 8:15). Stir within him (or her) a yearning—an unquenchable desire—to know You and live for You. Bring such heavy waves of conviction over him (or her) that he will find no rest until he (or she) has given in to Your relentless love. May he (or she) find the contentment and purpose that comes only from You.

Satan, you come only to steal, kill, and destroy (John 10:10). I forbid you from stealing my child, killing our hopes, and destroying the promise of salvation God has given our family. And by the authority of the name of Jesus, I command you to leave my family alone. Jesus, reveal Your presence to the enemy and to my child.

Please open my child's eyes and ears to the work of Your Holy Spirit. Give him (or her) a vision of Your grace and mercy because it's Your kindness that leads us to repentance (Rom. 2:4). Let him (or her) hear You calling his name, and bring other believers into my child's life to point him (or her) toward You.

I refuse to give up on my child because You refused to give up on me. When I was faithless, You remained faithful (2 Tim. 2:13). Even when Israel had given herself to other gods, You remained true to Your commitment of faithfulness (Hos. 2:2–23). Therefore, with boldness I come before Your throne and declare that I will stand in the gap on behalf of my child until the day of salvation (Ezek. 22:30).

Thank You, Lord Jesus, for the gift of eternal life. My deepest desire is to spend eternity in Your presence with my family at my side. May my dream—which I know is also Your dream—come true.

See also:

1-1. Magnifying the Lord
1-4. Praising God for His Creation
1-6. Yearning for More of Jesus
2-1. Thanking God for Sending Jesus
2-10. Thanking God for Choosing Me
3-5. Producing Endurance
3-8. Joining God in His Will
4-1. The Prayer of Salvation (Sinner's Prayer)
5-2. Peace for Worry
6-9. Unsaved Spouse
9-2. Unsaved Coworkers
11. Bringing in the Kingdom of God

5

WHEN YOU SEND YOUR CHILD TO SCHOOL

Apply your heart to instruction,
And your ears to words of knowledge.
(Prov. 23:12 NKJV)

Lord Jesus, with a heavy heart I send my child off to school. Away from the safety and security of our home my child faces countless challenges—mental, physical, emotional, and spiritual. As a parent, knowing this can be burdensome.

Please put my mind at ease. Remind me of Your deep love for my child—that I can cast all my cares upon You because *You* care for him (or her) (1 Peter 5:7). Because You are omnipresent, I can rest assured that You are with my child, directing and protecting him (or her), even when I cannot (Ps. 139:7–10).

Father God, bless my child with sound judgment. May his (or her) heart be one with Yours so he will walk in Your statutes and keep Your judgments (Ezek. 11:19–20). Instill within my child an innate sense of truth that will cause him (or her) to measure everything he hears against Your Word. "Your word is truth" (John 17:17 NKJV).

Bless my child with protection. Place a hedge around him (or her) (Job 1:10), and station Your angels to guard over him (Ps. 91:11). Shield his (or her) innocence from corruption, his mind from worldly values, his body from injury, his emotions from harm, and his spirit from iniquity.

Bless my child with a sound mind (2 Tim. 1:7). Empower him

(or her) to concentrate, listen to instructions, think clearly, speak wisely, and study judiciously. May he (or she) have the wisdom of Solomon, the heart of David, the perseverance of Joseph, and, above all, the mind of Christ (Rom. 12:2).

Bless my child with favor—from his (or her) friends to the adults You have appointed over him: teachers, administrators, coaches, and guidance counselors. Father God, as Your Son Jesus grew in wisdom and stature and in favor with God and men (Luke 2:52), may my child do likewise.

Holy Spirit, I trust You to be my child's counselor (John 14:26). Help my child to discern good from evil and make clear to him (or her) Your ways.

See also:

1-1. Magnifying the Lord
1-2. Meditating on His Omnipotence and Omnipresence
2-2. Thanking God for His Word
2-8. Thanking God for Supplying my Needs
2-9. Thanking God for His Protection
3-1. Guarding Purity
3-6. Learning Obedience
3-7. Developing Integrity
3-9. Building Faith and Trust
4-16. Fleeing Temptation
5-2. Peace for Worry
5-8. Courage for Fear

6

FOR THE FUTURE SPOUSE OF YOUR CHILD

Love suffers long and is kind; love does not envy; love does not parade itself, is not puffed up; does not behave rudely, does not seek its own, is not provoked, thinks no evil; does not rejoice in iniquity, but rejoices in the truth; bears all things, believes all things, hopes all things, endures all things.(1 Cor. 13:4–7 NKJV)

Father God, because the covenant of marriage is sacred and ordered by You (Mark 10:9), I pray for the future spouse of my child. According to Your Word, a marriage relationship should reflect Your holy relationship with the Church. So, Lord, order the steps of my child and his future spouse, that their marriage might glorify You just as You have revealed in Your Word (Eph. 5:25).

Lead my son to a woman whose love for You is unmatched by her love for him, a woman who's desire is to dwell in Your presence, a woman who speaks with wisdom and is full of trust, faith, and loyalty (Prov. 31:10–31).

Lead my daughter to a man whose love for You is unmatched by his love for her, a man who will love his wife just as he loves himself (Eph. 5:28), a man who will be her companion and best friend, a man who studies the Word, a man who is a good provider and loving father, a man who nourishes and cherishes her (Eph 5:29).

Lord, guard the purity of their relationship. May they flee youthful lusts and together pursue righteousness, faith, love, and peace (2 Tim. 2:22).

I place my trust in You, not to worry or fret over the decision my child makes concerning marriage. Marriage is a sacred vow, a holy matrimony, and only You, Lord, are able to bind together two lives according to Your purposes.

See also:

1-3. Cherishing God's Love
2-8. Thanking God for Supplying my Needs
2-10. Thanking God for Choosing Me
3-1. Guarding Purity
3-3. Bearing the Fruit of the Spirit
3-9. Building Faith and Trust
4-13. Dying to Selfishness
6-1. To Find a Wife
6-2. To Find a Husband

7

FOR THE PROTECTION OF YOUR CHILDREN

The LORD protects the simplehearted;
when I was in great need, he saved me.
(Ps. 116:6 NIV)

My children are so precious and innocent, Lord. They are the *simple*hearted.

Yet, the world they face today isn't so innocent. The world they face is *evil*-hearted, with impure and unholy motives. Danger lurks in the darkness, and I so easily fear for their safety.

I take solace in You, Lord, because You came to destroy the works of the devil (1 John 3:8). You said in Your Word, "do not fret because of evildoers" (Ps. 37:1 NKJV), so I cast all my fears upon You and Your protecting power (1 Peter 5:7).

You are my children's refuge and strength, an ever-present help in time of trouble—at school, at play, at home. (Ps. 46:1). Be a refuge, mighty God, and guard my children from physical harm, either by disease or injury. Be a refuge, keeping my children safe from accidents. Be a refuge, protecting my children from emotional and spiritual harm.

Father God, just as You kept Joseph safe in prison, baby Moses safe in a basket floating in the Nile, David safe from Goliath, and baby Jesus safe from Herod, I place my trust in You to keep my children safe.

Your favor is a shield that surrounds my children (Ps. 5:12), a hedge of protection that cannot be assailed by danger. Therefore, I confess my trust in You.

See also:

1-1. Magnifying the Lord
1-2. Meditating on His Omnipotence and Omnipresence
2-2. Thanking God for His Word
2-9. Thanking God for His Protection
3-1. Guarding Purity
3-6. Learning Obedience
3-7. Developing Integrity
3-9. Building Faith and Trust
5-2. Peace for Worry
5-8. Courage for Fear

8

WHEN YOUR CHILD FACES PEER PRESSURE

And do not be conformed to this world, but be transformed by the renewing of your mind, that you may prove what is that good and acceptable and perfect will of God. (Rom. 12:2 NKJV)

Lord Jesus, I see all the daily pressures my child faces: pressure from friends, classmates, coworkers, even teachers. Your Word says the devil is like a roaring lion, seeking someone to devour (1 Peter 5:8). It's only because of Your grace that anyone can avoid being devoured by sin. Jesus, please stand in the way of the devil coming near my child and enticing him to lead an unholy life, to take drugs and alcohol, to lie and cheat, to steal, to be involved in sexual perversion, or to commit violent acts.

May my child find the strength, by Your Holy Spirit, to be like the men of Judah, who "remained loyal to their king" when the rest of Israel went astray (2 Sam. 20:2 NKJV). Instill within my child the determination to desert the things of the devil rather than the things of God.

More important than being accepted by the "in" crowd is being accepted by You. Please make real to my child a love and acceptance that the world cannot duplicate. May You be the One my child seeks to please.

Please create within my child a thirst for more of You and Your Word. May Your Word be a lamp unto the feet of my child so that he can find his way through the darkness (Ps. 119:105). Bring into his path friends who are sold out for You and who will encourage him in his faith. Lord, may he become an active participant in our church.

Popular opinion isn't Your opinion, God, but it's not always easy for a young, impressionable person to see it that way. So make Your ways known to him. Give him a divine revelation of Your changeless nature (Heb. 13:8), and let him know You are with him every step of the way.

See also:

1-3. Cherishing God's Love
1-8. Worshiping in Spirit and Truth
2-2. Thanking God for His Word
2-7. Thanking God for Sending His Spirit
3-1. Guarding Purity
3-2. Growing in Holiness
3-5. Producing Endurance
3-7. Developing Integrity
3-9. Building Faith and Trust
5-2. Peace for Worry

8

RELATIONSHIPS

Whether we're willing to admit it or not, we all "need somebody to lean on." God created Adam, took one look at him, and said, "It is not good that man should be alone" (Gen. 2:18 NKJV). So He created Eve to be his companion.

Since then, men and women have had to learn how to live their lives in the context of human relationships. Apart from the occasional hermit, our relationships play a vital role in our very existence.

Every person is created with a God-shaped hole and a relationship hole. Jesus fills the first one, and our friendships fill the second. Where the two intersect, we "work out our salvation," as the apostle Paul would put it (Phil. 2:12).

God didn't create individuals, He created people. *Individuals* live their lives without concern for others; *people* live their lives in response to their relationship with others.

It's no wonder then that, devoid of relationships, a person feels lonely. Or that so many men and women yearn to share their lives with another person of the opposite sex. Or that we grieve when we lose a loved one. *God wired us for relationships!*

For that reason, Paul wrote that believers in Jesus are members of one body (1 Cor. 12). The body doesn't consist of an arm or a leg or a kidney. It functions properly as every part works together. The community that emerges in a local body of believers—our loving relationships with each other in the context of our life-giving relationship with Jesus Christ—should be the missing piece that the world longs for.

As inherently complex and perilous as they may be, our relationships serve as an effective gauge of our walk with God. A pattern of strained relationships may point to an area in our lives that needs further work. First John 4:20 tells us, "If someone says, 'I love God,' and hates his brother, he is a liar; for he who does not love his brother whom he has seen, how can he love God whom he has not seen?" NKJV.

Struggles in our friendships usually point to deeper issues that God may be working in our lives. So as you pray the prayers in this section, remember that the mountains you are facing in your relationships may also be mountains—deeper issues and behaviors—that God is trying to remove in your life.

1

HEALING STRAINED RELATIONSHIPS WITH PARENTS

"Honor your father and mother," which is the first commandment with promise: "that it may be well with you and you may live long on the earth." (Eph. 6:2–3 NKJV)

Father God, repeatedly in Scripture You instruct us to honor our parents. You even promise a long life to those who do so. But the hurt that has transpired between us makes obeying Your Word difficult: My head tells me to make things right, but my heart is hesitant.

I come before You, Lord Jesus, asking You to heal our relationship. Lift us out of the muck and mire of past offenses so we can communicate on the solid ground of grace and truth.

Give me the grace to forgive just as You have forgiven me (Eph. 4:32). Regardless of whether it was intentional, unintentional, severe, slight, or inexcusable, I release every offense into Your hands because *Your* yoke is easy and *Your* burden is light (Matt. 11:30). Breathe anew on my festering wounds with the breath of Your Holy Spirit; heal me so I can leave the past behind.

Open my eyes to see with truth what has caused the strain in our relationship. If there is any pride, rebellion, selfishness, hypersensitivity, or misunderstanding on my part, please reveal it to me so I can make it right.

In the same way, work in the hearts of my parents. Overwhelm them with Your love and compel them to forgive me just as You offer forgiveness to them (Matt. 6:12). Remove any blinders from their eyes that would prevent them from seeing clearly into the causes of our conflict.

By your Holy Spirit, may You restore us in humility and peace. But even if they choose not to be restored, I still choose to forgive. In honoring my parents I realize I am also honoring You (Eph. 5:21).

So grant me the courage to take the necessary steps in seeking forgiveness and being restored. May I have the boldness to approach them in all sincerity, meekness, and wisdom.

I know that everything works together for good, for those who are called according to Your purpose (Rom. 8:28). So even in this situation, I have faith that You will glorify yourself through it. I rest in peaceful confidence that you *will* do a good work. You are the Prince of Peace, and I give up all worry and anxiety about my relationship with my parents to You. Only You can ease the strain, so help me not to do it on my strength.

See also:

1-1. Magnifying the Lord
1-8. Worshiping in Spirit and Truth
1-9. Loving God's Will
2-3. Thanking God for the Cross and the Blood
2-4. Thanking God for His Grace and Mercy
3-3. Bearing the Fruit of the Spirit
3-6. Learning Obedience
4-11. Letting Go of Bitterness and Unforgiveness
4-12. Victory over Hatred
4-15. Finding Freedom from Rebellion
5-6. Calmness for Anger and Rage
5-9. Redemption in the Face of Tribulation

2

MENDING BROKEN FRIENDSHIPS

Therefore, as the elect of God, holy and beloved, put on tender mercies, kindness, humility, meekness, longsuffering; bearing with one another, and forgiving one another, if anyone has a complaint against another; even as Christ forgave you, so you also must do. But above all these things put on love, which is the bond of perfection. (Col. 3:12–14 NKJV)

Father God, You are the architect of relationships. You created Adam and Eve to commune with You. Yet, even that relationship—the very *first* relationship—broke down because of sin (Gen. 3). But through Your Son, Jesus, You have reconciled us to Yourself (Eph. 2:14–16).

Lord Jesus, just as You broke down the wall of separation between God and man, so I ask You to break down the wall that separates me from my friend. In the same way You are committed to me, I am committed to this relationship. So I ask you to please mend our broken friendship.

Despite the wounds that have been inflicted and the words that have been said, I sincerely desire to see our differences resolved. But apart from Your mediation, it won't happen. Tear down our strongholds of offense that have been erected and send the Counselor, the Holy Spirit, to counsel us (John 15:26) in putting on tender mercies, kindness, humility, meekness, longsuffering, and love, which is the bond of perfection (Col. 3:12–14).

Grant me the capacity to assess myself with sober judgment

(Rom. 12:3) so I can take responsibility for my actions and inaction. I repent of any pride that may have contributed to our separation. Please replace my selfishness with the fruit of the Spirit (Gal. 5:22–23).

Soften the heart of my friend. By the power of the Holy Spirit, speak into his life and show my friend anything he may have done to cause this division. May we humbly come to each other with the desire not only to be heard, but also to hear, understand, repent, and reconcile.

Lord, use the restoration of our relationship as a means to bring glory to Yourself. May we walk together, arm in arm, to show the world the power of Your love to overcome any conflict.

See also:

1-5. Acclaiming God's Majesty and the Beauty of Holiness
1-8. Worshiping in Spirit and Truth
2-1. Thanking God for Sending Jesus
2-3. Thanking God for the Cross and the Blood
2-4. Thanking God for His Grace and Mercy
3-2. Growing in Holiness
3-3. Bearing the Fruit of the Spirit
4-3. Overcoming Pride
4-11. Letting Go of Bitterness and Unforgiveness
5-6. Calmness for Anger and Rage

3

GRIEVING THE LOSS OF A LOVED ONE

But I do not want you to be ignorant, brethren, concerning those who have fallen asleep, lest you sorrow as others who have no hope. For if we believe that Jesus died and rose again, even so God will bring with Him those who sleep in Jesus. (1 Thess. 4:13 NKJV)

God, I am sad. My loved one is gone, forever. Your Word says those who believe in Your Son will have eternal life (John 3:16). But, right now, I still mourn: I am here, my loved one is there, and the distance between us seems immeasurable. I know we'll meet again in eternity with You. But, right now, that seems so far away.

I cry, but find no comfort. Time stands still while my emotions run amuck: One minute I feel OK, the next I am distraught.

No one understands my grief. Whom can I talk to? Whom can I share my life with? Like a leper, I feel like I'm an embarrassment to everyone I meet.

Every day brings a fresh awareness of my loss—another memory of times gone by, a memory nobody else remembers. Only me. Has anyone ever been this lonely, God?

My grief is ever present. I think about it all day, and I dream about it all night. Some dreams are sweet, but some are sordid nightmares. I wake up confused, then angry. Please reassure me that Your mercies are new every morning (Lam. 3:22–23).

At times, I feel like I'm going crazy. I'm bewildered, astonished. This can't be happening to me! It must be a bad dream. I'm going to wake up soon, right, God?

Are You there, God? Are You real? Can I ever trust You again? If so, please make Yourself known! Speak!

> Whom have I in heaven but You? And there is none upon earth that I desire besides You. My flesh and my heart fail; But God is the strength of my heart and my portion forever. (Ps. 73:25–26 NKJV)

Dear God, You are the strength of my heart. Even if You don't seem like You're there, I cast my eyes toward heaven, looking and waiting for Your return.

Purge me of my sorrow. By Your Spirit please ease my loneliness, relieve my grief, heal my guilt, calm my anger, and still my soul.

I want to remember my loved one, Lord, but I don't want to wallow in this pain. So make my memories sweet. Renew my spirit and give me patience with myself. Bring me a friend who will listen, and above all, fill me with hope so I won't grieve like those who have no hope.

I don't know how I would walk through this dark valley without Your Spirit guiding me and comforting me. Thank You for Your promise that You will never leave me nor forsake me (Heb. 13:5).

See also:

1-3. Cherishing God's Love
1-10. Rejoicing in the Face of Discouragement
2-4. Thanking God for His Grace and Mercy
2-5. Thanking God for the Resurrection of Christ
2-8. Thanking God for Supplying my Needs
3-5. Producing Endurance
5-3. Hope for Despair
5-6. Calmness for Anger and Rage
8-5. Easing Loneliness

4

FEELING ABANDONED AND REJECTED

He is despised and rejected by men, A Man of sorrows and acquainted with grief. And we hid, as it were, our faces from Him; He was despised, and we did not esteem Him. (Isa. 53:3 NKJV)

Father God, I reach out to You in my frail state of helplessness. Whether alone or in a crowd, the feelings of rejection and abandonment continue to gnaw away at my heart like a terminal disease.

It's a lonely feeling to be rejected. Waves of anger, discouragement, and self-doubt plague me at times. I feel like I'm dying inside. And sometimes I question whether my life is even worth living. Help me to sense Your presence, because in Your presence is fullness of joy (Ps. 16:11).

My greatest comfort is knowing that You were rejected, too. Your closest friends, Your family, even the people You sought to save abandoned You when You needed them most. Despite the love You showed and the lives You touched, they denied they knew You, they betrayed You, and they gave up on You. Then, as You hung on the cross, You were even forsaken by Your Father—almighty God (Matt. 27:46)!

Jesus, thank You for offering Yourself on the cross for my sins. You suffered the rejection of the Father so I wouldn't have to. Please give me a vision of God's unconditional love and acceptance. Make real to me Your promise that despite the rejection I experience here on earth, You will never leave me nor forsake me (Heb. 13:5).

Strengthen me to go on—to rise up from the ashes of my dejection and depression—and draw closer to You and Your love.

By the power of Your Spirit, I refuse to allow the enemy to sow seeds of unforgiveness, bitterness, vengeance, and hatred. Jesus, instill within me the grace to echo the same words You spoke on the cross: "Father, forgive them, for they do not know what they do" (Luke 23:34 NKJV).

Whether or not I am fully accepted again by those who have rejected me, I ask that You would fill me with Your *agape* love for them. May I not walk in the fear of rejection, but instead in Your perfect love, which casts out all fear (1 John 4:18).

Thank You that my value isn't dependent upon what other people think of me, but rather what *You* think of me. And nothing, NOTHING, can separate me from Your love (Rom. 8:35–39).

See also:

1-3. Cherishing God's Love
1-7. Adoring Christ, the Great "I AM"
1-10. Rejoicing in the Face of Discouragement
2-7. Thanking God for Sending His Spirit
2-10. Thanking God for Choosing Me
3-5. Producing Endurance
3-10. Finding Contentment
5-3. Hope for Despair
8-5. Easing Loneliness
10-5. Emotional Healing

5

EASING LONELINESS

My heart pants, my strength fails me; As for the light of my eyes, it also has gone from me. My loved ones and my friends stand aloof from my plague, and my relatives stand afar off. (Ps. 38:10–11 NKJV)

Lord Jesus, there are times in my life I feel so lonely. My family doesn't understand me, and my friends don't seem to care. Even when I'm around other people, I feel alone. It's a glum feeling, Lord, to think that no one else understands what I'm going through. Does anyone care? Is there someone I can count on, a companion, to help me overcome these difficult times?

Don't hide yourself from me now. Make real to me Your life-giving presence. You have made known to me the ways of life; You will make me full of joy in Your presence (Acts 2:28). Thank You for being a very present help in trouble (Ps. 46:1).

Speak to me, Lord. Help me to hear what You are saying in these times of silence. May I find comfort in the stillness of Your presence (Ps. 46:10). Please give me the grace to be patient in the quiet times, to learn from them, and to use them as a springboard to search out the deeper things of You.

Show me how to redeem my periods of silence like the great men and women in Your Word. Give me the anointing of Joseph, who bore his loneliness in slavery; of David, who lived alone while being pursued by Saul; of Moses, who climbed Mt. Sinai by himself while his people worshiped idols; of Paul, who forfeited his relationships to follow You; of Your Son, Jesus, who died on the cross while his best friends denied knowing him.

But You also gave Your servants a special friend, a trustworthy companion. To Moses, You gave Joshua. To David, You gave Jonathan. To Paul, You gave Timothy. Send me a friend, Lord. Send me someone I can pray with, talk with, laugh and cry with, someone who understands me and will help ease my loneliness.

Lord, these men encountered seasons of loneliness, but they saw them as opportunities to draw closer to You. So give me Your perspective. May I sense You drawing me closer to Yourself.

See also:

1-2. Meditating on His Omnipotence and Omnipresence
1-10. Rejoicing in the Face of Discouragement
2-1. Thanking God for Sending Jesus
2-7. Thanking God for Sending His Spirit
3-5. Producing Endurance
3-10. Finding Contentment
5-3. Hope for Despair
5-9. Redemption in the Face of Tribulation
8-4. Feeling Abandoned and Rejected

9

JOB AND CAREER

Have you ever said this: "If I didn't have to worry about finances my life would be great"? In our culture it has become increasingly fashionable to avoid work. In the coming decades, many business forecasters believe the amount of vacation and flex time employers offer will be more attractive to potential employees than the traditional pay and benefits package. All things being equal, the majority of us in the workplace would choose more leisure time over a higher salary package.

Every day, millions of us play Lotto—a form of government-sponsored gambling—in hopes of getting the big payoff so we can quit our jobs and spend the remainder of our lives living for ourselves. We seek what is referred to in layman's terms as *financial independence*.

Now making money—even lots of it—isn't sinful. Paul wrote, "the *love* of money is a root of all kinds of evil" (1 Tim. 6:10 NKJV, italics added). But doesn't it seem ironic that we want to make more while working less?

So why did God allow currency units and job markets to

develop along with the stress of paying our bills? In other words, why do we (or at least, most of us) have to work a job? Two reasons: (1) without a job we would become lazy; and (2) we wouldn't be forced to live by faith.

Interestingly enough, the punishment for Adam and Eve's sin was not only expulsion from the garden but also childbearing, sweat, and toil on the job (Gen. 3). You can blame the pain of childbirth and the aggravation of working on Adam and Eve!

But perhaps in God's plan, the leisure time Adam and Eve had in the Garden is what actually led them to sin in the first place. As children many of us were told, "An idle mind is the devil's workshop." Laziness, which is deplored throughout Scripture, offers us the time to follow our selfish and sin-prone inclinations. Ultimately, our sins drive us from God's presence and provision just as it did Adam and Eve.

Without faith it is impossible to please God (Heb. 11:6). But if we felt we had no need for God, to what extent would we be motivated to walk by faith? And how much would we grow in our faith? The mountains we are forced to scale in the workplace enable us to grow stronger. Hassling with a job search drives us to our knees because we realize the wrong job can set us back financially as well as provide a hardship we'd rather avoid. Sharing the good news of salvation with a coworker in the end strengthens us as well.

That said, the chance of retiring early because we have achieved financial independence borders on slim to none. But that's okay. Our jobs present prime opportunities for God to work in us and through us.

1

WISDOM AND GUIDANCE IN YOUR JOB SEARCH

Trust in the LORD with all your heart, And lean not on your own understanding; In all your ways acknowledge Him, And He shall direct your paths. (Prov. 3:5–6 NKJV)

Faithful God, like the children of Israel wandering through the desert, I seek Your promised land of provision. Give me an unmistakable sense of Your direction just as You did Israel when You led them with a cloud by day and a pillar of fire by night (Ex. 13:21).

Make straight before me a highway through the morass of job possibilities (Isa. 40:3). Open the doors You have ordained me to walk through and close the doors that don't fit into Your plan (Rev. 3:7). I confess my trust in You and commit myself to leaning on *Your* understanding, regardless of how enticing the job may appear. More important than income or benefits is being in the center of Your will.

At the same time, I stand on the promise of Your Word: "And my God shall supply all your need according to His riches in glory by Christ Jesus" (Phil. 4:19 NKJV). May I experience the abundance of Your provision and blessing just as You are able to make all grace abound toward me, that I, having all sufficiency in all things, may I have abundance for every good work (2 Cor. 9:8).

Your Word challenges me, "Ask and you will receive, that your joy may be full" (John 16:24 NKJV). I ask for a job that is tailored to my gifts, strengths, and passions. A job I look forward to going to. A job that not only operates as a source of income but as an outlet of ministry to my coworkers.

Because I trust You are directing my paths, I commit to walking by faith and not jumping into a job out of desperation or fear. Give me eyes to discern between good and best and the patience to wait for it.

"Behold, God is my salvation, I will trust and not be afraid; For the LORD GOD is my strength and song, And He has become my salvation" (Isa. 12:2 NASB).

See also:

1-9. Loving God's Will
2-2. Thanking God for His Word
2-8. Thanking God for Supplying my Needs
3-5. Producing Endurance
3-9. Building Faith and Trust
4-6. Triumphing over Greed, Indulgence, and Materialism
4-9. Giving God Control of Selfish Ambition
5-2. Peace for Worry
6-4. Financial Difficulties
6-8. Direction for the Future

2

UNSAVED COWORKERS

Walk in wisdom toward those who are outside, redeeming the time. Let your speech always be with grace, seasoned with salt, that you may know how you ought to answer each one. (Col. 4:5–6 NKJV)

Lord Jesus, Your love for even the most hardened reprobate is as wide and long and high and deep as Your great love for me (Eph. 3:18–19). Because You long to live with us for eternity, You're not willing that *any* should perish but that *all* should come to repentance (2 Peter 3:9).

Thank You for entrusting to me the opportunity of sharing the good news of salvation. You have brought a mission field into my own backyard! Send me with Your anointing into my workplace as a minister of Your redeeming love. I want to love people into Your kingdom.

Make me a channel of Your Holy Spirit in meeting people at the point of their need just as You did in Your earthly ministry. Stir within me words of knowledge, gifts of healing, and workings of miracles (1 Cor. 12:8–10) on my coworkers' behalf so they will encounter the power of Your love (Matt. 14:14). May the unhindered flow of Your gifts of the Spirit in my life yield fruit for Your Kingdom.

Orchestrate events in the lives of my associates that would compel them to reach out for You and schedule into my day divine appointments where we can discuss Your presence in those events

(Acts 17:26–27). May our conversations spring out of relationships so that they feel free to share in an atmosphere of safety and trust (Luke 5:30–32).

Without someone sharing the words of eternal life, they'll never know the freedom only You can bring. Anoint every word that proceeds from my mouth so that everything I say penetrates to the deepest longings of their hearts. Because it's Your kindness that leads us to repentance (Rom. 2:4), steer me away from debates and heated arguments that only drive people further away from You.

Set a guard over my lips (Ps. 141:3) so I'll know when to speak up and when to remain silent (Prov. 29:20). Open my ears so I can be a good listener.

I stake a claim for the kingdom of God and the cause of Christ in my work environment. In the name of Jesus, Satan, I bind you (Matt. 18:18) and all your influences at my job, and I forbid you from blinding the eyes of my coworkers from seeing the glorious light of the Good News that is shining upon them (2 Cor. 4:4). Jesus paid for their salvation with His blood (Rev. 5:9–10), so I loose the convicting power of the Holy Spirit and I lift up the name of Jesus that He would draw them to Himself (John 12:32).

See also:

1-3. Cherishing God's Love
1-4. Praising God for His Creation
2-1. Thanking God for Sending Jesus
3-4. Moving in the Gifts of the Spirit
3-8. Joining God in His Will
3-9. Building Faith and Trust
11-2. Sharing the Gospel
11-8. World Harvest

3

PROBLEMS WITH YOUR BOSS

And whatever you do, do it heartily, as to the Lord and not to men, knowing that from the Lord you will receive the reward of the inheritance; for you serve the Lord Christ. (Col. 3:23–24 NKJV)

Lord Jesus, I come before You seeking Your mediation to my conflict. Please help me sort through the issues of our struggle with humility and objectivity. But more important than determining who is right and who is wrong is the choice I make in how to respond to this problem. Use this as an opportunity to make me more like You.

You said, "Blessed are the peacemakers, For they shall be called sons of God" (Matt. 5:9 NKJV). Place within my heart the desire to do everything within my power to live peaceably with all people—including the person You have placed over me (Rom. 12:18). May my godly behavior compel my coworkers to call me a "son of God," and may I experience the reward of Your blessings because I have sought to make peace.

I stand on Your Word, which says, "Therefore humble yourselves under the mighty hand of God, that He may exalt you in due time, casting all your care upon Him, for He cares for you" (1 Peter 5:6–7 NKJV). I humble myself under Your mighty hand, knowing that no wrongdoing or unkind behavior escapes Your watchful eyes. I cast all my care upon You because *I know* You care for me. Lord, give me the patience to wait on Your divine timing to intervene.

I acknowledge to You that the way I submit to the authorities You have placed over me is the way I submit to *Your* authority (Num. 16:1–11). Although my superiors may oversee me, Lord, You are the one I work for. You are the one I seek to please (Col. 3:23–24). Therefore I will labor in my workplace with faithfulness, industriousness, and integrity regardless of the treatment I receive.

Fill me with Your love for my supervisor. May I see him/her through Your eyes of compassion. Give me insight into his/her life and the grace to be as patient with him/her as You are with me. Lord Jesus, I need Your strength to respond in love so that in every way my behavior will make You attractive (Titus 2:9–10 NIV).

By Your Spirit, remove the barriers that hinder effective communication. Open the ears of both parties that we would hear what the other is saying, and give us the discernment to identify what has brought us to this impasse. If there is a hardened heart on either side, soften it and bring us to reconciliation.

Sowing seeds of peace, I am confident You will bring to me a harvest of righteousness—that which pertains to goodness and justice.

See also:

1-8. Worshiping in Spirit and Truth
3-3. Bearing the Fruit of the Spirit
3-7. Developing Integrity
4-5. Defeating Gossip and Backbiting
4-8. Winning over Laziness
4-13. Dying to Selfishness
4-15. Finding Freedom from Rebellion
9-6. Favor

4

PROBLEMS WITH YOUR EMPLOYEES

Masters, give your bondservants what is just and fair, knowing that you also have a Master in heaven. (Col. 4:1 NKJV)

Almighty God, the only reason I serve in a position of authority is because You have placed me here (Rom. 13:1). "For there is no authority except from God, and the authorities that exist are appointed by God" (Rom. 13:1b NKJV). As Your appointed authority in my given scope of responsibility, I realize I not only answer to whomever rules over me, but I also answer to You (Col. 4:1). Therefore, I take very seriously the responsibility You have entrusted into my charge.

I desperately need Your wisdom to sort through the mixed emotions and conflicts that exist between my employee(s) and me. You promise in James 1:5 NKJV, "If any of you lacks wisdom, let him ask of God, who gives to all liberally and without reproach, and it will be given to him." So without any doubting, I look to You for guidance.

Give me the discernment to know when to apply the law and when to apply grace. May I be steadfast in the face of rebellion and courageous to do the right thing over the easy thing.

At the same time fill me with Your compassion toward those who answer to me. As a Christian and as a leader, I represent You. The power I have over my employees resembles the power You have over me. Give me the eyes to see my employee(s) as people created in Your image (Gen. 1:27), people You love just as much as me.

Prince of Peace, come permeate my workplace with Your presence. Bring clarity to our confusion and conciliation to our conflict. I commit myself to pursuing peace with all people, and holiness, without which no one will see the Lord (Heb. 12:14–15).

Reveal to me the redemptive lessons You are trying to work in my life through my employees. Prevent me from responding out of revenge, anger, or wounded pride, and work in me the humility to admit any of my shortcomings or faults that may have played a role in the tension that exists.

May Your love radiate through me, and may I model Your love for them.

See also:

1-3. Cherishing God's Love
1-8. Worshiping in Spirit and Truth
1-10. Rejoicing in the Face of Discouragement
2-4. Thanking God for His Grace and Mercy
3-3. Bearing the Fruit of the Spirit
3-5. Producing Endurance
4-9. Giving God Control of Selfish Ambition
4-11. Letting Go of Bitterness and Unforgiveness
4-13. Dying to Selfishness
5-6. Calmness for Anger and Rage

5

TRAVEL FOR BUSINESS

Have I not commanded you? Be strong and of good courage; do not be afraid, nor be dismayed, for the LORD your God *is* with you wherever you go. (Josh. 1:9 NKJV)

Heavenly Father, traveling on business exposes me to vulnerabilities I prefer not to face. Thank You for promising to be with me wherever I go (Josh. 1:9).

Dispatch Your angels to protect me from harm for "The angel of the LORD encamps all around those who fear Him, And delivers them" (Ps. 34:7 NKJV). I will not fear injury because You have promised to be with me (Isa. 43:1–2), holding me in the palm of Your hand (Isa. 51:16). Keep me alert while I'm driving, and place a hedge of protection (Job 1:10) around me to shield me from other drivers. Guide the judgment of the pilots who may fly me through the air and guard me against any mechanical failures.

The way I act when no one is looking is the real me. Although no one else may see me, You do. Shield my eyes from any impurity (Ps. 101:3). Show me when sin is lurking so I can run from it (2 Tim. 2:22). Keep in the forefront of my mind the family I have at home. According to Your Word, no temptation has overtaken me except such as is common to man, but You are faithful. You will not allow me to be tempted beyond what I am able, but with the temptation You will also make a way of escape, that I may be able to bear it (1 Cor. 10:13). Steer me away from any compromising situations, and show me the way of escape. Go before me into my motel room and fill it with Your manifest presence. May Your presence be so real that I would be embarrassed to follow my fleshly desires.

By the power of the Holy Spirit I put on the whole armor of God that I may be able to stand against the wiles of the devil. I buckle around my waist the belt of truth, with the breastplate of righteousness in place. I fit my feet with the readiness that comes from the gospel of peace and take up the shield of faith to extinguish the flaming arrows of the evil one. I put on the helmet of salvation and place in my hands the sword of the Spirit, which is the Word of God. And I seal it by praying in the Spirit on all occasions with all kinds of prayers and requests (Eph. 6:13–18a NIV). Thank You, Lord God, that in Christ Jesus, I am a more than a conqueror (Rom. 8:37).

When I feel lonely or homesick, please send Your ministering angels to comfort me (Heb. 1:14). Thank You for bearing my loneliness on the cross and giving me Your Holy Spirit. May my time away grow into a powerful opportunity for renewal as I make You my traveling companion.

See also:

1-2. Meditating on His Omnipotence and Omnipresence
1-5. Acclaiming God's Majesty and the Beauty of Holiness
1-8. Worshiping in Spirit and Truth
2-7. Thanking God for Sending His Spirit
2-9. Thanking God for His Protection
3-1. Guarding Purity
3-2. Growing in Holiness
3-7. Developing Integrity
4-16. Fleeing Temptation
5-3. Hope for Despair
8-5. Easing Loneliness

6

FAVOR

And the LORD gave the people favor in the sight of the Egyptians. Moreover the man Moses was very great in the land of Egypt, in the sight of Pharaoh's servants and in the sight of the people. (Ex. 11:3 NKJV)

Almighty God, throughout Scripture, a distinguishing mark of Your chosen people was the favor they found in the eyes of their superiors.

After Joseph was arrested under false charges, You showed him mercy by giving Him favor in the sight of the keeper of the prison. Joseph was then elevated to a place of authority (Gen. 39:21). When the children of Israel were departing Egypt, You gave them favor in the sight of the Egyptians. Soon their former captors blessed them with an abundance of possessions until Your chosen people had plundered them (Ex. 12:36).

As one of Your chosen people, I ask for favor in the eyes of my superiors. May You reward my faithfulness in the little with influence and ever-increasing responsibility (Matt. 25:21). Bless the work of *my* hands that my coworkers would see the imprint of *Your* hands and give You glory.

You promised Abraham that his descendants—Your chosen people—would be a blessing to all the peoples of the earth (Gen. 12:2–3). You fulfilled that promise in Jesus, and You continue to bless the peoples of the earth through those who are called by Your name. God, I ask that You would supply all my needs according to

Your riches in glory by Christ Jesus (Phil. 4:19), and then continue carrying out Your promise by making me a channel of financial blessing into the lives of others. May Your unmistakable blessing on my life—ultimately flowing into the lives of those around me—draw others closer to You (2 Cor. 9:8).

I acknowledge that every good gift and every perfect gift is from above and comes down from the Father of lights, with whom there is no variation or shadow of turning (James 1:17). May my presence bring pleasure and joy to those in authority over me just as Your presence does in my life.

See also:

1-4. Praising God for His Creation
1-7. Adoring Christ, the Great "I AM"
2-4. Thanking God for His Grace and Mercy
2-8. Thanking God for Supplying my Needs
3-7. Developing Integrity
3-10. Finding Contentment
4-6. Triumphing over Greed, Indulgence, and Materialism
9-8. Blessing for Your Company

7

PURPOSE IN THE WORKPLACE

> Therefore we also pray always for you that our God would count you worthy of this calling, and fulfill all the good pleasure of His goodness and the work of faith with power, that the name of our Lord Jesus Christ may be glorified in you, and you in Him, according to the grace of our God and the Lord Jesus Christ. (2 Thess. 1:11–12 NKJV)

Lord Jesus, You never intended for riches and prestige to quench my thirst for fulfillment. They merely serve as empty and bankrupt pursuits that leave me wanting more (1 Tim. 6:6–11). Rather, fulfillment comes from being in Your presence. "You show me the path of life. In your presence there is fullness of joy; in your right hand are pleasures forevermore" (Ps. 16:11 NRSV).

Sensitize me to Your life-giving presence. Reveal to me creative ways to glorify You and enjoy You in my workplace. Most of all, show me Your redemptive purpose for placing me here.

Because You have called me to be a minister of Your mercy and grace (1 Peter 2:9), please open wide the doors so I can make known to my coworkers the good news of salvation. May I use my spiritual gifts in the workplace to minister as a conduit of Your Holy Spirit. Direct me to those who are facing critical junctures and need to hear from You. Give me the anointed words to speak, and present opportunities for me to pray *with* people who wouldn't otherwise seek You. Place in my hands the keys that open the doors to closed hearts.

I realize that my true vocation is to serve as a tent-making minister, supporting myself through my job. You have given to me the ministry of reconciliation—reconciling people to Jesus Christ (2 Cor. 5:18–21). Open my spiritual eyes so I won't regard my peers according to the flesh—as people unconcerned about spiritual things—but according to Your Spirit—as people You died to save (2 Cor. 5:16).

In my *avocation*, reveal to me the wonders of Your creation. Stop me in the middle of my work to show me the depths of Your wisdom and love pertaining to my job responsibilities. Spur new and creative ideas that will bless my company and my company's customers.

Thank You that there is more to my life than earning a paycheck. Unveil before me my part in Your redemptive plan.

See also:

1-6. Yearning for More of Jesus
1-7. Adoring Christ, the Great "I AM"
1-8. Worshiping in Spirit and Truth
1-9. Loving God's Will
2-6. Thanking God for Making Me the Righteousness of God in Christ
2-10. Thanking God for Choosing Me
3-4. Moving in the Gifts of the Spirit
3-8. Joining God in His Will
3-10. Finding Contentment
4-8. Winning over Laziness
4-9. Giving God Control of Selfish Ambition
9-2. Unsaved Coworkers
9-6. Favor
11. Bringing in the Kingdom of God

8

BLESSING FOR YOUR COMPANY

So it was, from the time that [Potiphar] had made him overseer of his house and all that he had, that the LORD blessed the Egyptian's house for Joseph's sake; and the blessing of the LORD was on all that he had in the house and in the field. (Gen. 39:5 NKJV)

Lord God, I thank You for the many blessings You have bestowed upon Your chosen people. I rejoice that Your promise to Abraham to make him a great nation and that all the peoples of the earth would be blessed through his descendants (Gen. 12:2–3) extends even through me (Rom. 11:17-24)! Please bless me and then make me a blessing to others.

Just as You blessed the employers of Jacob (Gen. 30:27) and Joseph (Gen. 39:5), so I ask that You would bless my employer. May the abundance they experience be so great that it drives them to respond, "This must be the hand of God!"

Dear God, bless my company for my sake. Bless us with financial prosperity. Bless us with stamina and stability. Give us creative ideas promoting effectiveness and efficiency that place us on the cutting edge of our industry. May those in leadership make decisions based upon the wisdom of God rather than the knowledge of men. "For God's foolishness is wiser than human wisdom, and God's weakness is stronger than human strength" (1 Cor. 1:25 NRSV).

At the same time I ask that You would steer my company away from greed and selfish ambition. May our vision for business extend beyond padding the bottom line. Fill us with compassion for the poor, and give us hearts of generosity so we, too, can be a blessing to others. Raise up a standard of integrity that inspires coworkers to labor with honesty and forthrightness.

Cultivate an atmosphere of mutual care and concern between workers and management that would position us as the model of goodwill and cooperation. May we truly become a family.

Establish around the perimeter of our employees a hedge of protection from sickness and disease. "The blessing of the LORD makes one rich, And He adds no sorrow with it" (Prov. 10:22 NKJV).

Most of all, bless us with an impartation of Your manifest presence. Give us a glimpse of Your beauty and majesty that hearts would be changed and Your Spirit would be poured out on all people. Make our work environment fertile ground for a harvest of souls.

> Let Your work appear to Your servants, And Your glory to their children. And let the beauty of the LORD our God be upon us, And establish the work of our hands for us; Yes, establish the work of our hands. (Ps. 90:16–17 NKJV)

See also:

1-3. Cherishing God's Love
1-5. Acclaiming God's Majesty and the Beauty of Holiness
2-4. Thanking God for His Grace and Mercy
2-8. Thanking God for Supplying my Needs
3-9. Building Faith and Trust
4-3. Overcoming Pride
4-6. Triumphing over Greed, Indulgence, and Materialism
4-9. Giving God Control of Selfish Ambition
9-6. Favor
11-3. Compassion for the Poor and Needy

10

SICKNESS AND DISEASE

"At least we have our health!"

How many times have you heard the aforementioned response after someone has experienced a severe hardship? Most of us can weather nearly any storm as long as we have the stamina to withstand it. On the heels of a bankruptcy, we can do without a new car or a family vacation. After being laid off from our job, we can tighten the financial belt a little tighter and skip going out to eat as much. But what do you do when your body is buffeted by sickness and pain? How do you keep your hope intact? Wherein lies your secondary line of defense?

The mountains we face that take the form of sickness or disease touch us where we are most vulnerable. The ruthlessness of terminal illness or the relentlessness of chronic sickness can batter even the strongest man or woman into submission. Where can a person go to elude it?

It's no wonder Jesus' earthly ministry focused, to a great extent, on meeting the physical and emotional needs of the people of his day. By healing the sick, Jesus touched people where God's love intersects with human experience. What many call a "power encounter" drew people closer to the Father.

Jesus healed people because He loved them. "And when Jesus went out He saw a great multitude; and He was moved with compassion for them, and healed their sick" (Matt. 14:14 NKJV). He didn't heal them because He owed it to them, He did it simply because He had compassion for them.

The good news is Jesus hasn't changed. "Jesus Christ is the same yesterday, today, and forever" (Heb. 13:8 NKJV). He is still moved with compassion when He sees us in pain, and He still heals today just as He did two thousand years ago.

We pray for healing, believing that God can and does heal. We relentlessly pursue Him with our request until we receive an answer. But we also trust Him. Faith and prayer move God, but the decision to heal still remains with Him. Sometimes God heals on this earth. Sometimes He doesn't. And we don't always know why. That's part of the mystery of God. Yet without prayer, *no one* would have the hope of encountering His divine intervention to remove their mountains of sickness and disease.

1

SUPERNATURAL HEALING

Surely He has borne our griefs And carried our sorrows; Yet we esteemed Him stricken, smitten by God, and afflicted. But He was wounded for our transgressions, He was bruised for our iniquities; The chastisement for our peace was upon Him, And by His stripes we are healed. (Isa. 53:4–5 NKJV)

Almighty God, I come before You in the name of Jesus, knowing that You hear my prayer and care about my needs (Rom. 8:32). Your love is stronger than my sin (Rom. 8:38–39). Your faithfulness is greater than my suffering (Lam. 3:23). Your power is mightier than my sickness (Ps. 103:3). You are *Jehovah-Rapha*, the God who heals me (Ex. 15:26).

I present myself to You asking that You would touch me. Breathe into me Your breath of life (Gen. 2:7). May the creative power of Your life-giving Holy Spirit course throughout my body and make me whole again.

Lord Jesus, You bore *my* griefs. You carried *my* sorrows. You were esteemed stricken, smitten by God, and afflicted. But You were wounded for *my* transgressions. You were bruised for *my* iniquities. You took the chastisement for *my* peace upon Yourself, and by Your stripes *I am healed* (Isa. 53:4–5).

Your blood is more than sufficient to cleanse me, heal me, and secure my salvation (Heb. 9:13–14). Cover me with Your precious blood.

Your Word says, "Confess your trespasses to one another, and pray for one another, that you may be healed" (James 5:16 NKJV). Examine my heart. Convict me and purge me of any sin that hinders the flow of Your healing power. I resolve to come clean with all my sin so that You would wash me and restore my body.

Throughout Your earthly ministry, You demonstrated Your love and compassion by healing the physical and emotional infirmities of men and women just like me (Matt. 14:14). And everyone who touched You was made well. Lord Jesus, I reach out to touch even the hem of Your garment that You would heal me just as You healed them (Mark 5:27–28).

I place my confidence in Your love, Your faithfulness, and Your power to overcome any ailment, disorder, or malady. And I rejoice in advance as I anticipate Your intervention on my behalf.

I cast *all* my cares upon You because I know You care for me (1 Peter 5:7).

See also:

1-1. Magnifying the Lord
1-2. Meditating on His Omnipotence and Omnipresence
1-3. Cherishing God's Love
2-1. Thanking God for Sending Jesus
2-2. Thanking God for His Word
2-3. Thanking God for the Cross and the Blood
2-4. Thanking God for His Grace and Mercy
2-5. Thanking God for the Resurrection of Christ
2-7. Thanking God for Sending His Spirit
3-9. Building Faith and Trust
4. Sin
5-8. Courage for Fear
10. Sickness and Disease
11-7. Outpouring of Signs and Wonders

2

WISDOM AND DISCERNMENT FOR MEDICAL PROFESSIONALS

> When Jesus heard that, He said to them, "Those who are well have no need of a physician, but those who are sick." (Matt. 9:12 NKJV)

God all-wise, You are the Great Physician. You forgive all my iniquities, You heal all my diseases (Ps. 103:3). All wisdom, knowledge, and truth belong *to* You and come *from* You (Dan. 2:20–23). As I subject myself to the care of doctors, nurses, technicians, and other medical personnel, I ask You to endow them with Your wisdom, knowledge, and truth. Give them discernment into my condition that transcends human logic. Remove any barriers that would hinder them from being directed by Your Spirit.

Just as You filled the tabernacle with Your glory (Ex. 40:34–35) and established Your throne on the mercy seat (Ex. 25:22), so I invite You to fill my room. Take Your place beside me and reassure me with Your presence.

Rub the hands of my doctors and nurses with Your divine Balm of Gilead (Jer. 8:22). Guide them as they care for me and *through* their hands, heal my body.

Your Word says:

> Because you have made the LORD, who is my refuge, Even the Most High, your dwelling place, No evil shall befall you, Nor shall any plague come near your dwelling; For He shall give

His angels charge over you, To keep you in all your ways. (Ps. 91:9–11 NKJV)

Surround me with Your angels to protect me from any infection or harm. May they keep my caregivers alert to any abnormalities in my condition.

But above all, I resolve not to place my trust in any physician, but in You, the Great Physician (2 Chron 16:12). All healing comes through You, all wisdom comes from You, and anything good that results in my recovery begins with You (James 1:17). So I entrust myself into Your care, knowing that You are in ultimate control.

See also:

1-1. Magnifying the Lord
1-2. Meditating on His Omnipotence and Omnipresence
1-3. Cherishing God's Love
1-9. Loving God's Will
2-2. Thanking God for His Word
2-8. Thanking God for Supplying my Needs
2-9. Thanking God for His Protection
3-9. Building Faith and Trust
5-2. Peace for Worry
10-3. Recovery from a Medical Procedure

3

RECOVERY FROM A MEDICAL PROCEDURE

About this same time, Hezekiah got sick and was almost dead. He prayed, and the LORD gave him a sign that he would recover. (2 Chron. 32:24 CEV)

Father God, I come to You in the name of Jesus, thanking You for the expertise You give men and women in the medical profession to be instruments of Your healing. All knowledge and skill begins *with* You and results *from* You. "Every good gift and every perfect gift is from above, and comes down from the Father of lights, with whom there is no variation or shadow of turning" (James 1:17 NKJV).

Your Word says that if I make You my refuge, then no evil shall befall me, nor shall any plague come near my dwelling; for You shall give Your angels charge over me, to keep me in all my ways (Ps. 91:9–11). Surround me with Your protection to guard me from any infection or further complication.

Just as Hezekiah prayed and You gave him a sign that he would recover, so I ask You to grant me *complete* recovery from my infirmity. And more so, please provide a sign to show those around me that You are intimately involved in my life and their lives as well. May my quick recovery astound the doctors, nurses, technicians, medical personnel, and visitors in such a divine way they will say, "I have seen the hand of God!"

Rather than while away my time on meaningless drivel, use my recovery as an opportunity to strengthen my inner person

(Eph. 5:16). Fill my room with songs of worship and praise. Avert my eyes from the television and into the riches of Your Word. Stir my spirit so I can be an intercessor for the needs of others and for the furthering of Your kingdom. I am determined to make the most of every opportunity (Col. 4:5).

I choose to put on the garment of praise for the spirit of heaviness (Isa. 61:3). I choose to be receptive to the good You are working in my life as a result of my recuperation (Rom. 5:3–5).

And when my healing is complete, give me the words to articulate to those around me of Your saving and healing power. In every way, may my recovery bring You glory.

See also:

1-1. Magnifying the Lord
1-2. Meditating on His Omnipotence and Omnipresence
1-3. Cherishing God's Love
2-1. Thanking God for Sending Jesus
2-2. Thanking God for His Word
2-3. Thanking God for the Cross and the Blood
2-4. Thanking God for His Grace and Mercy
2-5. Thanking God for the Resurrection of Christ
3-5. Producing Endurance
3-9. Building Faith and Trust
5-3. Hope for Despair
5-9. Redemption in the Face of Tribulation
10-2. Wisdom and Discernment for Medical Professionals
10-6. Protection from Sickness and Disease

4

GOD'S COMPASSION AND HEALING FOR SICK CHILDREN

And behold, one of the rulers of the synagogue came, Jairus by name. And when he saw [Jesus], he fell at His feet and begged Him earnestly, saying, "My little daughter lies at the point of death. Come and lay Your hands on her, that she may be healed, and she will live." (Mark 5:22–23 NKJV)

Heavenly Father, thank You that I can come to You knowing You are my Father and I am Your child. "The LORD is like a father to his children, tender and compassionate to those who fear him" (Ps. 103:13 NLT). Your love for Your children far exceeds that of any earthly father or mother.

Children are a heritage from You (Ps. 127:3). They are gifts You loan us for a season until they are old enough to care for themselves. Lord I lift up this little child before You and ask that You would have mercy on him. Like the daughter of the Centurion, take this child by the hand and raise him up out of this sickbed (Mark 5:21–42).

I stand on Jesus' promise in John 14:12–14 (NKJV):

Most assuredly, I say to you, he who believes in Me, the works that I do he will do also; and greater works than these he will do, because I go to My Father. And whatever you ask in My name, that I will do, that the Father may be glorified in the Son. If you ask anything in My name, I will do it.

Just as You healed . . . just as You promised . . . just as Your word stands forever . . . I ask in the name of Jesus that You would fulfill Your Word and accomplish through my prayer Your greater works. "For with God nothing will be impossible" (Luke 1:37 NKJV). Heal this child that the Father may be glorified in the Son.

I come against a spirit of infirmity in the name of Jesus and I say, "Child, you are loosed from your infirmity" (Luke 13:11–12). Jesus, please touch this child with Your healing hands and bless him (Mark 10:16).

Utilize this circumstance as a benchmark in the spiritual life of this child. May this draw him closer to You, and may it serve as a testimony to Your love and faithfulness.

See also:

1-1. Magnifying the Lord
1-2. Meditating on His Omnipotence and Omnipresence
1-3. Cherishing God's Love
1-4. Praising God for His Creation
2-1. Thanking God for Sending Jesus
2-3. Thanking God for the Cross and the Blood
2-4. Thanking God for His Grace and Mercy
2-5. Thanking God for the Resurrection of Christ
2-7. Thanking God for Sending His Spirit
3-9. Building Faith and Trust
5-2. Peace for Worry
5-8. Courage for Fear
7-7. For the Protection of Your Children

5

EMOTIONAL HEALING

> But to you who fear my name, the Sun of Righteousness will rise with healing in His wings. And you will go free, leaping with joy like calves let out to pasture. (Mal. 4:2 CEV)

God of all comfort, how can I forget all the benefits You offer to those who call on Your name? You forgive all my sins and heal all my diseases. You redeem my life from the pit and crown me with love and compassion. You satisfy my desires with good things so that my youth is renewed like the eagle's (Ps. 103:2–5 NIV). I lay my life before You, seeking Your redeeming and renewing touch.

The weight of carrying my pain has drained me of strength and hope. Jesus, You said, "Take My yoke upon you and learn from Me, for I am gentle and lowly in heart, and you will find rest for your souls. For My yoke is easy and My burden is light" (Matt. 11:29–30 NKJV). Exchange my wearisome yoke for Your easy yoke. I release to You my heavy burdens—hurt, discouragement, hopelessness, anger, despair—and I take on Your light burdens.

You shed Your blood on the cross not only for my forgiveness and physical healing, but for my emotional healing as well (Matt. 8:16–17). Your Word declares that You heal the brokenhearted and bind up their wounds (Ps. 147:3). Lord, bind up my griefs, sorrows, and hurts and re-create them into reminders of Your redeeming love. Heal my broken heart and make me whole again through Your precious blood.

Rather than erasing it from my memory, give me the eyes to see my past *through* the blood of Jesus Christ. Show me that in my darkest moment of hurt and pain, You were there—weeping with me, hurting for me, strengthening me, and encouraging me to go on. During my long, dark night of the soul, when I walked through the valley of the shadow of death, You walked beside me (Ps. 23:4), ensuring I wouldn't experience more heartache than I could endure (1 Cor. 10:13).

But no matter how dark the night may become, I know Your mercies are new every morning. "Through the LORD's mercies we are not consumed, Because His compassions fail not. They are new every morning; Great is Your faithfulness" (Lam. 3:22–23 NKJV). To every night there is a morning, and to every hurt, there is healing.

Sun of righteousness, arise with healing in Your wings and shine the light of Your love into the darkest corners of my life. Release me from this pain so I can leap with joy like a calf let out to pasture (Mal. 4:2). Transform my ashes into beauty. Apply the oil of joy to my broken heart. Clothe me with the garment of praise for the spirit of heaviness (Isa. 61:3). Redeem my past and use it to shape me into the person You designed me to be.

See also:

1-3. Cherishing God's Love
1-7. Adoring Christ, the Great "I AM"
1-10. Rejoicing in the Face of Discouragement
2-4. Thanking God for His Grace and Mercy
3-5. Producing Endurance
4-11. Letting Go of Bitterness and Unforgiveness
4-12. Victory over Hatred
5-3. Hope for Despair
5-6. Calmness for Anger and Rage

6

PROTECTION FROM SICKNESS AND DISEASE

> Because you have made the LORD, who is my refuge, Even the Most High, your dwelling place, No evil shall befall you, Nor shall any plague come near your dwelling; For He shall give His angels charge over you, To keep you in all your ways. (Ps. 91:9–11 NKJV)

Lord Jesus, I rejoice that *all* authority has been given to You in heaven and on earth (Matt. 28:18). No principality or power, no human institution or invention, no infirmity or illness can prevail against You (Eph. 1:21). I also rejoice that You have given Your disciples power and authority over all demons, and to cure diseases (Luke 9:1–2).

Therefore, in the name of Jesus, I rebuke the spirit of infirmity and forbid it from prevailing over me (Luke 13:11). From the common cold to terminal cancer, Lord, strengthen my immune system. I stand on the promise of God's Word that because I have made the Lord my refuge, no evil shall befall me, nor shall any plague come near my dwelling (Ps. 91:9–11). Lord, dispatch Your angels to encamp around my dwelling and protect me from harm (Ps. 34:7).

Your Word declares:

> If you diligently heed the voice of the LORD your God and do what is right in His sight, give ear to His commandments and keep all His statutes, I will put none of the diseases on you which I have brought on the Egyptians. For I am the LORD who heals you. (Ex. 15:26 NKJV)

Because I have the righteousness of God in Christ and I belong to You, I ask that no disease would come near me. For You are the Lord who heals me.

May the magnitude of Your presence around me be so great that nothing will be able to touch me except that which comes from You. "For You, O LORD, will bless the righteous; With favor You will surround him as with a shield" (Ps. 5:12 NKJV).

Because my body is a temple of the Holy Spirit (1 Cor. 3:16–17), steer me away from destructive habits that make me vulnerable to weakness and infirmity. I want to worship You, body, soul, and spirit.

May the hedge of protection (Job 1:10) You have placed around me serve as a testimony to those of Your power, Your protection, and Your love.

See also:

1-2. Meditating on His Omnipotence and Omnipresence
1-8. Worshiping in Spirit and Truth
2-3. Thanking God for the Cross and the Blood
2-9. Thanking God for His Protection
3-5. Producing Endurance
5-1. Rest for Sleeplessness
5-2. Peace for Worry
7-7. For the Protection of Children

7

TERMINAL ILLNESS

And the word of the LORD came to Isaiah, saying, "Go and tell Hezekiah, 'Thus says the LORD, the God of David your father: "I have heard your prayer, I have seen your tears; surely I will add to your days fifteen years."'" (Isa. 38:4–5)

Almighty God, You have made the heavens and the earth by Your great power and Your outstretched arm. Nothing is too difficult for You (Jer. 32:17). You are the Creator and sustainer of life (Ps. 139:13–16). In Your eyes nothing is truly terminal because *all* sickness and disease bow down before You.

Lord Jesus, You were wounded for *my* transgressions, You were bruised for *my* iniquities. The chastisement for *my* peace was upon You, and by Your stripes, *I am healed* (Isa. 53:5). May Your healing blood flow through my veins.

You are the resurrection and the life (John 11:25), and through the power of the Holy Spirit You were raised from the dead on the third day to reign over the penalty of sin: death (1 Peter 3:18). Your Word says, "But if the Spirit of Him who raised Jesus from the dead dwells in you, He who raised Christ from the dead will also give life to your mortal bodies through His Spirit who dwells in you" (Rom 8:11 NKJV). Because the Spirit dwells in me, I call upon that same power that raised Jesus from the dead. Reverse this progression of death upon my mortal body, and infuse me with Your resurrection life.

Just as You granted King Hezekiah's request to extend his life by fifteen years (Isa. 38:4–5), so I ask for an extension on mine. I don't want to take my final breath until I have fulfilled every plan You have for me. Give me time to share the good news of salvation with my friends and loved ones. Open the doors into the lives of others so I can minister the power of Your love. May my testimony of healing serve as a means of glorifying You.

"He asked life from You, and You gave it to him—Length of days forever and ever" (Ps. 21:4 NKJV). As long as I have breath in me, I will persist in asking for Your deliverance. I refuse to go down without a struggle because I know that all things are possible to him who believes (Mark 9:23). *Jesus, I believe.*

See also:

1-1. Magnifying the Lord
1-2. Meditating on His Omnipotence and Omnipresence
1-7. Adoring Christ, the Great "I AM"
1-10. Rejoicing in the Face of Discouragement
2-3. Thanking God for the Cross and the Blood
2-4. Thanking God for His Grace and Mercy
2-5. Thanking God for the Resurrection of Christ
3-5. Producing Endurance
3-9. Building Faith and Trust
5. Stress
10-1. Supernatural Healing
10-2. Wisdom and Discernment for Medical Professionals
11-7. Outpouring of Signs and Wonders

8

CHRONIC SICKNESS

And suddenly, a woman who had a flow of blood for twelve years came from behind and touched the hem of His garment. For she said to herself, "If only I may touch His garment, I shall be made well." But Jesus turned around, and when He saw her He said, "Be of good cheer, daughter; your faith has made you well." And the woman was made well from that hour. (Matthew 9:20–22 NKJV)

Dear Jesus, I am so thankful no obstacle is too great or too small for Your boundless grace. From Your eternal perspective, all diseases, sicknesses, and ailments are of equal size and importance. Your earthly ministry demonstrated that the power of Your love overcomes every problem, every person, every pain.

Like the woman who had the flow of blood for twelve years, I know that if I could just touch the hem of Your garment, I would be healed (Matt. 9:20–22). Your Word says, "Wherever He entered into villages, cities, or in the country, they laid the sick in the marketplaces, and begged Him that they might just touch the hem of His garment. And as many as touched Him were made well" (Mark 6:56 NKJV). Lord, hear my prayer as I reach out for You. Make Your presence known so I can touch the hem of Your garment. Even if I have to wait twelve years like this woman, I am determined to seek out Your healing presence.

When You encountered the man at the pool of Bethesda who had been an invalid for thirty-eight years, You asked him, "Do you want to be made well?" And by Your grace You raised him up from his bed even though he failed to answer Your question. But Lord, I answer Your question with a resounding "Yes!" Yes, I want to be made well. Yes, I want to be raised up from this bed of chronic sickness so I can shout, dance, and sing praises to Your name (John 5:5–8)!

If You can heal the woman with the flow of blood after twelve years, You can heal me. If You can heal the crippled man at the pool of Bethesda after thirty-eight years, You can heal me. If You can make the blind see, the leper cleansed, the deaf hear, and the dead raised, You can breathe Your resurrection life into my mortal body. Lord Jesus, reach into my temporal world and touch me with the eternal.

Remove from me any doubt that You are either unable or unwilling to heal (Mark 1:41). Because faith comes from You (Rom. 10:17), instill within me an immovable, unshakable confidence in Your goodness and Your power.

See also:

1-1. Magnifying the Lord
1-2. Meditating on His Omnipotence and Omnipresence
1-6. Yearning for More of Jesus
1-10. Rejoicing in the Face of Discouragement
2-4. Thanking God for His Grace and Mercy
3-9. Building Faith and Trust
10-1. Supernatural Healing
10-2. Wisdom and Discernment for Medical Professionals

9

WHEN GOD DOESN'T HEAL

Oh the depth of the riches both of the wisdom and knowledge of God! How unsearchable are His judgments and unfathomable His ways! For who has known the mind of the LORD, or who became His counselor? For from Him and through Him and to Him are all things. To Him be the glory forever. Amen. (Rom. 11:33–34, 36 NASB)

You are the infinite God. Your wisdom is far deeper and Your ways far higher than mine (Rom. 11:33). You set the sun, moon, and stars in their place because You are awesome in power (Jer. 31:35). By giving Your Son to die on the cross for my sins, You demonstrated a love that is unequaled (Rom. 5:8). So I know that nothing—no infirmity or disease—lies beyond the reach of Your wisdom, power, and love.

Although I have diligently sought Your deliverance, my healing still isn't complete. In my limited understanding, I don't know why, because You are able to do exceedingly, abundantly above all that I ask or think (Eph. 3:20).

But one thing I do know: You are God. Your works are perfect, and *all* Your ways are just. You are faithful, upright, and You do *no* wrong (Deut. 32:4). Because You are God and I am a mere human, understanding the mystery of Your ways is impossible (1 Cor. 2:7–9).

Just like the many men and women of faith who died before receiving the fulfillment of Your promises, I will diligently seek

Your intervention, cling to Your assurance of faithfulness, and look forward to a better place:

> These all died in faith, not having received the promises, but having seen them afar off were assured of them, embraced them and confessed that they were strangers and pilgrims on the earth. But now they desire a better, that is, a heavenly country. Therefore God is not ashamed to be called their God, for He has prepared a city for them. (Heb. 11:13, 16 NKJV)

Like the man who pestered his friend to all hours of the night for food, so I will persist in seeking my healing until I see You face-to-face (Luke 11:5–8). I will continue to hold on in faith believing You will heal me, but because You are God, I will leave the results with You.

I may not understand Your ways, but I trust Your heart. And until I am healed—either here or in the hereafter—open my eyes to Your immeasurable, matchless, all-sufficient grace. May Your strength be made perfect in my weakness. Until that day I will gladly boast in my infirmities, that Your power may rest upon me (2 Cor. 12:9).

See also:

1-2. Meditating on His Omnipotence and Omnipresence
1-3. Cherishing God's Love
1-5. Acclaiming God's Majesty and the Beauty of Holiness
1-9. Loving God's Will
1-10. Rejoicing in the Face of Discouragement
3-5. Producing Endurance
3-9. Building Faith and Trust
5-9. Redemption in the Face of Tribulation

11

BRINGING IN THE KINGDOM OF GOD

Have you ever wondered what makes "The Hallelujah Chorus" such a powerful song? Every Christmas, people flock to hear Handel's oratorio *The Messiah.* This beautiful work concludes with its defining moment. As the triumphant introduction begins, the listeners—Christian and non-Christian alike—rise to their feet in reverence to hear the choir sing a song of only four lines. Strangely enough, this unconscious response takes place without any prompting from the conductor or orchestra. Yet, if ever a song was written that echoes the choirs of angels in heaven, surely it is "The Hallelujah Chorus."

Apart from serving as a tool of worship, the words of this particular song express the very heart and ultimate will of God. Sandwiched between repeated "hallelujahs" Handel quotes directly from Revelation 11:15: "The kingdoms of this world have become the kingdoms of our Lord and of His Christ, and He shall reign forever and ever!"

What the audience identifies with in some spiritual sense, either wittingly or unwittingly, is God's ultimate goal of transforming the kingdoms of this world into the kingdom of God.

Jesus' central message in the Gospels was the kingdom of God (Matt. 4:17). When He exorcised a demon (Matt. 12:28), or sent out his disciples to carry on His ministry (Luke 9:1–2), it was done with the furthering of the kingdom in mind.

The synonymous terms *kingdom of God* or *kingdom of heaven* mean the rule and reign of God. The kingdom is not so much a boundary like a country, but rather God's dominion in human hearts. Jesus ushered in the beginning of the kingdom of God here on earth, but left his disciples to finish the job.

In the Lord's prayer, Jesus instructed His disciples to pray the kingdom of God into existence, "Your kingdom come. Your will be done On earth as it is in heaven" (Matt. 6:10 NKJV). As God's kingdom is established here on earth, His will is done as well. Jesus urged His disciples in Matthew 6:33, "But seek first the kingdom of God and His righteousness, and all these things shall be added to you" NKJV.

The prayers in this section are devoted to seeing God's ultimate will—His rule and reign—accomplished. God's heart beats for the lost. Like a father estranged from his child, He longs to be united with His children. Without hesitation we know God's chief concern is to reconcile all people to Himself (2 Cor. 5:18–19).

So who or what stands in the way of God's will being done? We do. Granted, God's will *will* eventually be accomplished. But what prevents it from happening sooner rather than later is our commitment to seeking first His kingdom. God has willingly chosen to use the prayers of His people as a vehicle to accomplish His will.

If you ever wanted to know for certain what the will of God is . . . if you ever wanted to pray for the issues on God's heart . . . if you ever wanted to play a part in seeing "the kingdoms of this world" become "the kingdoms of our Lord and of His Christ," then pray these prayers.

1

REVIVAL IN THE CHURCH

> If My people who are called by My name will humble themselves, and pray and seek My face, and turn from their wicked ways, then I will hear from heaven, and will forgive their sin and heal their land. (2 Chron. 7:14 NKJV)

Heavenly Father, You promise in Your Word that if we humble ourselves and admit our need for You; if we earnestly seek Your face more than we seek Your hand; if we turn from all habits and conditions of the heart that draw us away from You and pursue a lifestyle intent on pleasing You, then we *will* hear from heaven. You *will* forgive our sin, and You *will* heal our land.

I come before You and confess that what hinders Your kingdom from being established on earth is not the actions of this evil world, but the inaction of Your slumbering church. Our prayerlessness exposes our deep-rooted pride because it implies that we don't need Your involvement in our lives. Forgive us, Father, for calling ourselves by Your name while living independent of You.

Far too often we pick and choose which elements of You we really want while discarding the rest: We want Your salvation but not Your sanctification—the formation of Your character and behavior (1 Peter 1:15–16). We want the forgiveness in the blood of Jesus without the cross of dying to ourselves (Luke 9:24). We seek to know You based solely upon the power of Your resurrection *without* sharing in Your sufferings (Phil. 3:10–11). Father, forgive us for accepting You on our terms and not Yours; for seeking

Your *Holy* Spirit while ignoring our sin; for focusing our attention on the gift more than the Gift-giver.

Jesus, You said You will build Your church and the gates of hell will not prevail against it (Matt. 16:18). But we have become more concerned with our church buildings than building Your church. Please forgive us for constructing walls of protection from the very people You died to save (Rom. 5:8). We have hoarded the truth of Your Word and failed to share it freely with others (Matt. 10:8). We have wrongly cursed the darkness rather than embrace the light.

Jesus, make us holy, cleansing us by the washing with water through the Word. May You present to the Father a glorious church, without stain or wrinkle or any other blemish (Eph. 5:25–27 NIV). Purify Your church so that nothing impedes the flow of Your Spirit in us, among us, and through us. Shake our foundations of hay and stubble. Dear God, do whatever it takes to bring Your people to repentance—beginning with me.

May *Your* kingdom come and *Your* will be done on earth as it is in heaven (Matt. 6:10). The prophet Malachi foretold the day when the hearts of the fathers would be turned to their children and the hearts of the children to their fathers (Mal. 4:6). Father God, restore the hearts of Your children to You. May we ache for the salvation of this world because You ache for them to be reconciled with You.

Lord, awaken the sleeping giant! May the fire that consumes our impurities also light the flame of revival. We long to see Your Spirit poured out on all flesh, just as the prophet Joel foretold (Joel 2:28). We beg of You, by Your grace and mercy—give us a visitation from heaven (Isa. 44:3).

Your ways are so much higher than ours (Isa. 55:9). We want anything and everything You have for us—even if it strays outside our preconceived ideas of how You work (Eph. 3:20). Shake us from our cold formalism, and empower us to live lives of worship in spirit and truth (John 4:23–24).

Jesus, You said, "Blessed are those who hunger and thirst for righteousness, For they shall be filled" (Matt. 5:6 NKJV). Stir within Your people a hunger and thirst for righteousness that we would be filled. Heed our prayer for more of You, and immerse us in the river of Your Holy Spirit (Ezek. 47).

See also:

1-5. Acclaiming God's Majesty and the Beauty of Holiness
1-6. Yearning for More of Jesus
1-8. Worshiping in Spirit and Truth
2-3. Thanking God for the Cross and the Blood
2-7. Thanking God for Sending His Spirit
3-1. Guarding Purity
3-2. Growing in Holiness
3-8. Joining God in His Will
4. Sin
11. Bringing in the Kingdom of God

2

SHARING THE GOSPEL

For I am not ashamed of the gospel of Christ, for it is the power of God to salvation for everyone who believes, for the Jew first and also for the Greek. (Rom. 1:16 NKJV)

Lord Jesus, Your name is above all names. At Your name, every knee will bow and every tongue confess that You are Lord (Phil. 2:9–11). In Your name is healing (Acts 4:30). But most of all, in Your name is salvation. Thank You that anyone who calls upon Your name will be saved (Rom. 10:13). Out of gratitude for our salvation and in obedience to Your Word (Mark 16:15), we, Your church, commit ourselves to sharing the gospel—the good news—of Jesus Christ.

Infuse us with courage to walk in the fear of God rather than the fear of man. Your Word says, "In the fear of the LORD there is strong confidence" (Prov. 14:26). Grant Your people a revelation of how small we are compared to Your matchless power and might. If You are for us, who can be against us (Rom. 8:31)?

"For out of the abundance of the heart the mouth speaks" (Matt. 12:34 NKJV). Jesus, flood our hearts with so much love for You and those around us that we wouldn't be able to hold back from sharing the good news. May Your Word in our hearts be like a fire shut up in our bones that we can no longer contain (Jer. 20:8).

Because Your Word will not return void (Isa. 55:11), place *Your* words into our mouths. May we have the boldness to say *what* You want us to say *when* You want us to say it. Give us the discernment to speak with insight into the hurts and needs of people's lives.

We want to be moved with Your compassion for people who don't yet know You (Mark 6:34). Draw Your body into redemptive relationships of mutual trust and honesty. Cultivate in us the grace to share Your good news with all sensitivity and humility (Col. 4:5–6). Because we must earn the right to be heard, guard Your people from sin and negative habits that would disqualify us from sharing (1 Cor. 9:27).

Everything we have and everything we are belongs to You. Therefore, use the spiritual gifts You have bestowed upon us for Your good use (1 Cor. 12). Holy Spirit, inspire us with creative ideas for using our strengths to share the gospel.

Lord, I'm not content to sit idly by, watching You move in this world with grace and power. My heart's desire is to be used by You. Draw me into Your divine plan that I would be an asset for the kingdom.

See also:

1-2. Meditating on His Omnipotence and Omnipresence
1-3. Cherishing God's Love
2-1. Thanking God for Sending Jesus
3-4. Moving in the Gifts of the Spirit
4-1. The Prayer of Salvation (Sinner's Prayer)
4-8. Winning over Laziness
5-8. Courage for Fear
9-2. Unsaved Coworkers
9-7. Purpose in the Workplace
11-1. Revival in the Church
11-8. World Harvest
11-9. Dispatching Laborers into the Field

3

COMPASSION FOR THE POOR AND NEEDY

For I was hungry and you gave Me food; I was thirsty and you gave Me drink; I was a stranger and you took Me in; I was naked and you clothed Me; I was sick and you visited Me; I was in prison and you came to Me . . . Assuredly, I say to you, inasmuch as you did it to one of the least of these My brethren, you did it to Me. (Matt. 25:35–36, 40b NKJV)

Father God, You are rich in grace (Eph. 1:7) and abounding in mercy (Ps. 103:8). Even before the foundation of the world was laid, You chose to lavish us with Your great love (Eph. 1:4-8). You didn't just *tell* us You loved us, You *showed* us by giving Your only Son Jesus to die on the cross for our sins so we could have eternal life (John 3:16). Thank You.

In the same way, our love for others is evidence of Your love in us (1 John 4:7–8). Lord, fill us with that same love that is rich in grace—giving to others what they *don't* deserve, and abounding in mercy—not giving to others what they *do* deserve.

Convict us when we are deceiving ourselves by loving only in word but failing to love as You do—in deed and truth (1 John 3:18). Never are we more like You than when we give—in finances, in time, in actions—without expectation of anything in return. By Your Spirit working in us and Your love working through us, inspire Your people to model lifestyles of generosity.

Father, forgive us when we fail to live up to the standard of Your love. You call us to defend the cause of the weak and fatherless and to maintain the rights of the poor and oppressed (Ps. 82:3 NIV). May we escape the judgment of Sodom that was destroyed for neglecting the poor and needy (Ezek. 16:49).

Lord, we repent for allowing greed and materialism to seduce us. We have stockpiled Your blessings and neglected to share them freely with others (Gen. 12:2). Purge Your church of the passions and desires of this fallen world: the lust of the flesh, the lust of the eyes, and the pride of life (1 John 2:16).

Forgive us for being more occupied with ourselves than the needs of others. For separating evangelism from concern for the poor. For severing word from deed, and faith from works (James 2:17). Gracious God, renew within Your church a compassion for the underprivileged and a vision for reaching our communities for the kingdom. Spur creative ideas to empower the less fortunate. Stir within us a generosity in finances, in time, and in actions that the world through us would experience the love that comes from God.

No one is deserving of Your grace and mercy. Freely we have received, so freely we give (Matt. 10:8). May Your promise in Isaiah 58:10 be fulfilled in this generation that will break loose the barriers to worldwide revival: "Give your food to the hungry and care for the homeless. Then your light will shine in the dark; your darkest hour will be like the noonday sun" (CEV).

See also:

1-3. Cherishing God's Love
1-8. Worshiping in Spirit and Truth
2-4. Thanking God for His Grace and Mercy
2-8. Thanking God for Supplying my Needs
3-10. Finding Contentment
4-6. Triumphing over Greed, Indulgence, and Materialism
4-13. Dying to Selfishness

4

UNITY IN THE BODY OF CHRIST

I in them and you in me. May they be brought to complete unity to let the world know that you sent me and have loved them even as you have loved me. (John 17:23 NIV)

Father, Son, and Holy Spirit, in the expression of Your love there is perfect unity (John 17:22). If You weren't in one accord with each other, we would be nothing more than mortal pawns in a divine game of chess. But because of Your perfect love, we can know the unity of the Spirit in the bond of peace (Eph. 4:3).

Lord Jesus, it must break Your heart to see Your church divided. Your body was broken once for all when You were crucified in our place (1 Cor. 11:24). Forgive us for needlessly crucifying You again through division and dissension. Our disunity exposes our deep level of carnality (1 Cor. 3:3–4). May we, Your church, answer Your prayer to be one, just as the Father, Son, and Holy Spirit are one (John 17:20–21).

Please forgive us for our spiritual arrogance in assuming our church, denomination, or theological perspective has a corner on God. You are so much bigger than any person can conceive or institution contain. We have wrongly emphasized our distinctives over lifting up the name of Jesus. In so doing, we are guilty of dividing the body of Christ (1 Cor. 1:12–13).

Even when we acknowledge our bond in Christ, we so often contradict our claims by failing to worship together and work alongside other Christians. Forgive us for neglecting our brothers and sisters who worship or believe slightly differently yet remain as committed to You and the gospel as we do.

Break down the walls of prejudice that prevail according to race, skin color, income, disability, and gender because in Christ "there is neither Jew nor Greek, there is neither slave nor free, there is neither male nor female," for we are all one in Christ Jesus (Gal. 3:28).

Lord, purify our local congregations of petty squabbles and disagreements. Cleanse us of backbiting, criticism, outbursts of anger, and other sins that hinder Your Spirit from flowing among us.

Grant us a revelation and appreciation of the redemptive gifts each person, congregation, denomination, and theological perspective brings to Your church. We need Your wisdom to discern the difference between what is essential, what is cultural, and what is inherently sinful. We need Your humility, that we would submit to one another according to one anothers' strengths.

Lord, birth within Your people a burden to lay their weapons down and gather together as One. For there is only one body, one Spirit, one Lord, one faith, one baptism, and one God and Father of all, who is above all, and through all, and in all (Eph. 4:3-6).

Jesus, You are our peace (Eph. 2:14). You have made us one with the Father, now make us one with each other.

See also:

1-3. Cherishing God's Love
1-8. Worshiping in Spirit and Truth
2-7. Thanking God for Sending His Spirit
3-3. Bearing the Fruit of the Spirit
4-3. Overcoming Pride
4-9. Giving God Control of Selfish Ambition
4-13. Dying to Selfishness
4-15. Finding Freedom from Rebellion

5

GUIDANCE FOR CHURCH AND PASTORAL LEADERSHIP

Obey those who rule over you, and be submissive, for they watch out for your souls, as those who must give account. Let them do so with joy and not with grief, for that would be unprofitable for you. Pray for us; for we are confident that we have a good conscience, in all things desiring to live honorably. (Heb. 13:17–18 NKJV)

Great and mighty God, in an age where leaders in the religious and secular arenas fall from grace with regularity and grave consequences, we desperately need Your direction.

Guide by Your Spirit the men and women who lead Your church: ministry heads, denominational officials, pastors, and elders. Grant them a common vision to prepare this world for Your return. May sharing Your love with the hurting and spreading the good news of salvation be their all-consuming passion.

Raise up leaders—men and women of integrity—who count it more important to build *Your* kingdom than serve themselves (Matt. 6:33). Grace Your leaders with the wisdom from above that is pure, peaceable, gentle, willing to yield, full of mercy and good fruits, without partiality and without hypocrisy (James 3:17). Impart to them sound judgment and common sense to an uncommon degree.

Guard the purity of those who lead so that after preaching to others of Your transforming power, they themselves would not be disqualified (1 Cor. 9:27). Instill within them a deep fear of God and a fervent hatred of sin. Most of all, anoint them with the power of Your Holy Spirit. Give them the words to teach, preach, and explain the mystery of the gospel with all boldness and without fear of reprisal (Eph. 6:19). May they preach Jesus Christ (2 Cor. 4:5).

God all-wise, thank You for giving Your church apostles, prophets, evangelists, pastors, and teachers. Through their ministry we are equipped, edified, unified, and made complete (Eph. 4:11–13).

Birth within them an unrelenting desire to empower every believer into ministry (1 Peter 2:9). Use them to raise up an army of believers released into a world held captive by sin, that they would embark on missions of mercy and evangelism.

Grow Your leaders at every level of responsibility—international, national, and local—deeper in prayer (Acts 6:4). May they be men and women dedicated to seeking Your face (Ps. 24:1–6). Inspire in them a vision to transform our church buildings into houses of prayer (Matt. 21:13).

Last of all, generate within Your people the character to follow without being a burden (Heb. 13:17). May we submit to our leaders with all humility because You resist the proud but give grace to the humble (1 Peter 5:5). Through the prayers of the saints and the love of the Spirit, may Your leaders be refreshed to continue the path set before them (2 Cor. 1:10–11).

See also:

1-9. Loving God's Will
2-2. Thanking God for His word
3-1. Guarding Purity
3-8. Joining God in His Will
4-15. Finding Freedom from Rebellion
11-6. Sound Judgment for Government and Public Officials

6

SOUND JUDGMENT FOR GOVERNMENT AND PUBLIC OFFICIALS

I urge, then, first of all, that requests, prayers, intercession and thanksgiving be made for everyone—for kings and all those in authority, that we may live peaceful and quiet lives in all godliness and holiness. This is good, and pleases God our Savior, who wants all men to be saved and to come to a knowledge of the truth. (1 Tim. 2:1–3 NIV)

Lord God, no one is able to stand in the way of Your ultimate will. The elements of nature—weather and the change in seasons—as well as *human* nature—the unfolding of historic events and the appointment of men and women to their places of authority—are subject to Your desires. Even the decisions of those You have appointed over us are not beyond the reach of Your influence and power. "The king's heart is in the hand of the LORD, Like the rivers of water; He turns it wherever He wishes" (Prov. 21:1 NKJV).

In obedience to Your Word, I make requests, prayers, intercession, and thanksgiving on behalf of those You have placed in authority over me (1 Tim. 2:1–3).

Lord, breathe a fresh wind of Your Holy Spirit over the political leaders of this nation. Blow through our capitols, parliaments, assemblies, and legislatures, convicting them of sin. Reveal to our decision-makers Your all-consuming love for them and bring them to a saving knowledge of Jesus Christ. May we enter a new era of religious freedoms based not upon a change in laws, but rather a change in human hearts.

Just as You blessed King Solomon's request for wisdom, so I ask the same on behalf of our governing authorities: grant them an understanding heart to govern Your people and discern good from evil (1 Kings 3:9). Guide their decisions that we may live peaceful and quiet lives in all godliness and holiness (1 Tim 2:2). Instill within them a strong sense of justice, hearts of compassion, a hunger for righteousness, and an uncompromising measure of integrity. Incline their hearts toward fulfilling *Your* purposes (Rev. 17:17).

I recognize all governing authorities that exist were instituted by You and are instruments of Your will (Rom. 13:1). Therefore, I respect them, honor them, and subject myself to their authority (Rom. 13:5–7). Whenever we, Your people, are tempted to gossip or complain, stir our hearts to intercede for them through prayer instead.

Last of all, thank You for giving them to us. May You use our authorities to establish Your government here on earth (Isa. 9:7).

See also:

1-2. Meditating on His Omnipotence and Omnipresence
1-9. Loving God's Will
2-7. Thanking God for Sending His Spirit
2-8. Thanking God for Supplying my Needs
3-1. Guarding Purity
3-8. Joining God in His Will
3-9. Building Faith and Trust
4-15. Finding Freedom from Rebellion
11-5. Guidance for Church and Pastoral Leadership

7

OUTPOURING OF SIGNS AND WONDERS

And these signs will follow those who believe: In My name they will cast out demons; they will speak with new tongues; they will take up serpents; and if they drink anything deadly, it will by no means hurt them; they will lay hands on the sick, and they will recover." (Mark 16:17–18 NKJV)

Almighty God, throughout Scripture and at various times in the history of Your church, You used power encounters to affirm that Jesus was the divine Son of God (John 20:30–31) and to bring glory to Yourself (John 11:4). Signs and wonders were an opportunity for Your *real* world to invade our *un*real world. And in the process, You touched people with an unmistakable love that defied human logic (Mark 1:41–45).

Jesus, You promised that signs would follow those who believe (Mark 16:17–18). Furthermore, You said, "Most assuredly, I say to you, he who believes in Me, the works that I do he will do also; and greater works than these he will do, because I go to My Father" (John 14:12 NKJV).

But since the first generation of Your church, we have yet to see the completion of Your promise. Lord, what prevents Your words from being fulfilled is not Your *unwillingness*, but rather our *worldliness*. Show us where our worldly, fleshly perspective resides and how it hinders the flow of Your Spirit.

We know You were unable work many miracles among Your own family and friends because of their unbelief (Matt. 13:58).

Two thousand years later, we still struggle with the same problem. Please forgive us—Your very family and friends—for doubting Your ability and willingness to demonstrate the power of Your love. Lord, may we never become so familiar with You that You are unable to work freely among us.

Because faith comes from You, please increase our faith so we will believe—really believe—in Your ability to invade our temporal world with Your eternal power (Mark 9:24). Give us spiritual ears that are sensitive to the leading of Your Spirit and the boldness to step out and rely on You to intervene.

Weed out any selfish motives that would attempt to manipulate signs and wonders in order to titillate our senses and draw attention to ourselves. May our undying focus be to share *Your* love with a hurting world and to further *Your* kingdom.

More than seeking the manifestations of Your power, we seek You. Jesus, we invite You to make Your presence known among us so we can know You (Phil 3:10–11). May You use the demonstration of Your power through Your church so that Your kingdom will come and Your will will be done on earth just as it is in heaven (Matt. 6:10).

See also:

1-1. Magnifying the Lord
1-8. Worshiping in Spirit and Truth
2-5. Thanking God for the Resurrection of Christ
2-7. Thanking God for Sending His Spirit
3-3. Bearing the Fruit of the Spirit
3-4. Moving in the Gifts of the Spirit
3-9. Building Faith and Trust
5-8. Courage for Fear
10. Sickness and Disease

8

WORLD HARVEST

Ask of Me, and I will give You The nations for Your inheritance, And the ends of the earth for Your possession. (Ps. 2:8)

Father in heaven, we know Your heart breaks over lost souls. Your word says You're not willing that any should perish (2 Peter 3:9); that You take no pleasure in the death of the wicked (Ezek. 18:23); that You desire to see all people saved and come to a knowledge of the truth (1 Tim 2:4).

You have challenged Your church to ask of You and You would give the nations for our inheritance and the end of the earth for our possession (Ps. 2:8). Lord Jesus, give us the nations as our inheritance. Grant us the ends of the earth for our possession that the kingdoms of this world would become the kingdoms of our Lord and of His Christ (Rev. 11:15). Move upon the people of this world—the people you died to save—with the conviction of Your Holy Spirit (Rom. 5:8).

Till the fallow ground of human hearts so that the seeds of the gospel may be sown into fertile soil. "But he who received seed on the good ground is he who hears the word and understands it, who indeed bears fruit and produces: some a hundredfold, some sixty, some thirty" (Matt. 13:23 NKJV). Open the ears for people to hear and understand the mystery of the gospel. Saturate the seeds with Your living water, and nurture them in the light of Your love that there would be a great, end-time harvest like none the world has ever known.

I come against the god of this age who has blinded people from the light of the gospel of the glory of Christ. In the name of Jesus I forbid you from the use of all your deceptive devices (2 Cor. 4:4). The weapons of our warfare are not carnal but mighty in God for pulling down strongholds. Therefore, I cast down arguments and every high thing that exalts itself against the knowledge of God, and I bring every thought into captivity to the obedience of Christ (2 Cor. 10:4–5).

Holy Spirit, orchestrate world events that will expose the bankruptcy of all other religious pursuits, and open the eyes of the people of this world to the preeminence and beauty of Jesus (Ps. 90:17). Pare away the misconceptions that hide His lovingkindness behind the caricature of dead religion.

Jesus, I pray that they, being rooted and established in love, may have power, together with all the saints, to grasp how wide and long and high and deep is Your love, and to know this love that surpasses knowledge—that they may be filled to the measure of all the fullness of God (Eph. 3:17b–19 NIV).

Lord, You have placed a longing for eternity in the hearts of all people (Eccl. 3:11). Satisfy this yearning with the eternal life that only comes through Jesus Christ (John 14:6).

See also:

1-3. Cherishing God's Love
2-1. Thanking God for Sending Jesus
3-4. Moving in the Gifts of the Spirit
5-8. Courage for Fear
9-2. Unsaved Coworkers
9-7. Purpose in the Workplace
11-2. Sharing the Gospel
11-9. Dispatching Laborers into the Fields

9

DISPATCHING LABORERS INTO THE FIELD

> Then [Jesus] said to them, "The harvest truly is great, but the laborers are few; therefore pray the Lord of the harvest to send out laborers into His harvest. (Luke 10:2 NKJV)

Lord Jesus, You said You would build Your church and the gates of hell would not prevail against it (Matt. 16:18). We rejoice at what You are accomplishing in this world to fulfill Your word. Only through the power of Your Holy Spirit could You perform such mighty works through Your people.

The harvest truly is great, but the laborers are few (Luke 10:2). Lord, move upon Your church to labor in the harvest and carry out Your command,

> Go therefore and make disciples of all the nations, baptizing them in the name of the Father and of the Son and of the Holy Spirit, teaching them to observe all things that I have commanded you; and lo, I am with you always, even to the end of the age. (Matt. 28:19–20 NKJV)

May Your mandate to make disciples of all nations be completed in this generation.

Burn in the hearts of Your church a passion to employ every means available to share the gospel. May we channel every resource at our disposal toward reaching the lost: our time, our finances, our security, our prayer . . . our hearts.

Lord Jesus, You said that whoever does not forsake all that he has cannot be Your disciple (Luke 11:33). Help us to avert our focus from our selves, our reputations, our lifestyles, and onto You and the task set before us. Give us a foretaste of the joy that comes from leaving the safety and comfort of the ninety-nine to save the one (Matt. 18:12).

The fields are *already* ripe for harvest (John 4:35). Open our eyes to see where it is. Grant wisdom to our mission leaders so they will send out workers into the most strategic locations. Birth a unified vision between the various mission organizations and national religious leaders so they can divide and conquer the strongholds of the enemy.

It's Your kindness that leads us to repentance (Rom. 2:4). Therefore, stir up creative ideas that will enable Your workers to communicate the love of Jesus in a compelling manner. At the same time, well up within those staying at home hearts of generosity to support them.

May those of us called to remain at home not be content living as vicarious observers. Open our eyes to the mission field in our own neighborhoods so we can continue Your work.

Lord, deep within our hearts we hear You asking, "Whom shall I send, And who will go for us?" May each believer in one voice answer, "Here am I! Send me" (Isa. 6:8).

See also:

1-9. Loving God's Will
2-1. Thanking God for Sending Jesus
3-8. Joining God in His Will
4-13. Dying to Selfishness
5-8. Courage for Fear
11-2. Sharing the Gospel

10

THE SECOND COMING OF CHRIST

And this gospel of the kingdom will be preached in all the world as a witness to all the nations, and then the end will come. (Matt. 24:14 NKJV)

Lord God, You have been so good to us: You supply our needs according to Your riches in Christ Jesus (Phil. 4:19); You satisfy our desires with good things (Ps. 103:5); You fill us with purpose and contentment (1 Tim. 6:6–8). Your boundless grace and new mercies never come to an end.

But this world is not our home. We desire a better place—a heavenly country (Heb. 11:16). We yearn for the day when Your glory is fully revealed in all the earth (Isa. 40:5) and Satan is forever crushed under our feet (Rom. 16:20).

Most of all, dear Jesus, we long for the day when we will be united with You. The day when we will no longer say "Know the Lord," because we *will* know the Lord (Jer. 31:33–34). The day when You will wipe away every tear from our eyes (Rev. 21:4).

We long to go to a place prepared for us (John 14:2). A place where there will be no more death, no more sorrow, no more crying, and no more pain, because the former things of this fallen world will have passed away. Forever (Rev. 21:4).

Jesus, we pray for the gospel of the kingdom to be preached in all the world as a witness to all the nations, so that the end *will* come (Matt. 24:14).

So Lord we pray, "Maranatha—come, Lord Jesus" (1 Cor.

16:22). We may not know the day or the hour of Your return (Mark 13:32), but we are resolute to live in anticipation of spending eternity in Your embrace.

See also:

1-1. Magnifying the Lord
1-5. Acclaiming God's Majesty and the Beauty of Holiness
1-6. Yearning for More of Jesus
2-1. Thanking God for Sending Jesus
2-3. Thanking God for the Cross and the Blood
2-5. Thanking God for the Resurrection of Christ
2-10. Thanking God for Choosing Me
3-10. Finding Contentment
5-3. Hope for Despair
10-9. When God Doesn't Heal
11-8. World Harvest

BENEDICTION

Have you ever heard someone play a song on the piano but stop before the song was completed—then, for a while afterward you felt incomplete until the song was resolved? What you needed was closure. Without it, the song would continue to ring on endlessly in Your head.

You may have noticed that none of the prayers in this book concluded with that handy device we often use to bring resolution to our prayers. We call it an "Amen." You can add them if you like—there's nothing wrong with saying it—but they were purposely left out because prayer shouldn't stop with an "Amen."

Long after we're done *formally* praying, our prayerful attitude should continue. Repeatedly we are encouraged in Scripture to keep on praying:

- "Then [Jesus] spoke a parable to them, that men always ought to pray and not lose heart" (Luke 18:1 NKJV).
- "Continuing steadfastly in prayer" (Rom. 12:12 NKJV).
- "Continue earnestly in prayer" (Col. 4:2 NKJV).

- "Praying always with all prayer and supplication in the Spirit" (Eph. 6:18 NKJV).
- "Night and day praying exceedingly" (1 Thess. 3:10 NKJV).
- "Pray without ceasing" (1 Thess. 5:17 NKJV).

All too often, when we bring closure to our prayer, we leave God at the dinner table, at the altar, in our prayer closet. However, the prayer that moves mountains is the kind that continually intercedes before the Father long after the "formal" prayer is over. By leaving these prayers "unresolved," we hope You will find them ringing endlessly in Your head long after this book has been placed back on the shelf.

But to bring closure to this book, we did decide to leave one "Amen" in. We conclude with a benediction from the Bible that is our prayer for you:

> Now to Him who is able to keep you from stumbling,
> And to present *you* faultless
> Before the presence of His glory with exceeding joy,
> To God our Savior,
> Who alone is wise,
> Be glory and majesty,
> Dominion and power,
> Both now and forever.
> —Amen.
> (Jude 24–25 NKJV)

APPENDIX

THE TEN QUALITIES OF A MOUNTAIN-MOVING PRAYER

1. Rooted in Worship

Because this was discussed in Chapter 2 it will be explained here only briefly. We enter into God's presence with praise and thanksgiving. The psalmist wrote, "Come before His presence with singing . . . Enter into His gates with thanksgiving, / And into His courts with praise" (Ps. 100:2b, 4a). Our arms are outstretched in adoration of Him rather than open hands in expectation of a request fulfilled. Prayer is more than running down a list of "I wants."

Beginning with worship enables us to align our perspectives with God's. When Jesus instructed his disciples how to pray, He told them to begin by saying, "Our Father who art in heaven, hallowed be Thy name." *Hallowed* means simply, "holy, complete, and set apart." God doesn't need to be reminded He is holy. But we do.

Prayer that moves mountains is rooted in worship.

2. Unfettered Through Confession of Sin

Jesus died on the cross to cleanse us from every sin. However, unconfessed sin can stand between us and an unhindered relationship with God. James 5:16 reminds us, "Confess your trespasses to one another, and pray for one another, that you may be healed." James wasn't writing to the unsaved, he was writing to the saved.

Unconfessed sin—in the life of the believer and to a much greater extent in the life of the unbeliever—places a wall of separation between God and us. But true confession of sin tears it down. The prayers listed in Chapter 3 and Chapter 4 are designed to aid you in entering God's presence with a pure and clean heart.

Prayer that moves mountains is unfettered through confession of sin.

3. Expressed in Specifics

Did you ever stop to consider that every day God gives us new insights into His mercy? Lamentations 3:22–23 reminds us that God's mercies are new *every* morning. A beautiful sunset, a quick recovery from a head cold, or an unexpected compliment from your boss are just a few examples of God's mercies that are new every morning. In response we should return the favor to God by blessing Him in new ways. Every day, try to find some new means of expressing your love to Him. Just as He is specific in showing us His new mercies, so should we be specific in giving Him our praise. If you love Him, don't just tell Him you love Him, tell Him *why* you love Him.

The same principle is true when coming to Him with our requests. One day as Jesus was departing Jericho, the cries of two blind men could be heard over the din of the accompanying crowd. Walking to their side of the road, Jesus asked them a very important question: "What do you want Me to do for you?" (Matt. 20:32 NKJV). They didn't give some generic catchall answer like, "We want You to *be* with us." No. They replied, "We want our eyes to be opened."

Jesus asks us the same question in prayer: "What do you want

Me to do for you?" Nothing is more uninspiring in prayer than something like, "God, I pray that you will be with Sally." In all reality, that prayer is answered because God already *is* with Sally. What Sally really needs is victory over depression. For this reason, Chapters 5 through 10 are designed to aid you in praying specifically for stressful feelings, marriages and families, children, relationships, jobs and career, and sickness and disease.

Prayer that moves mountains is expressed in specifics.

4. Focused on the Kingdom

Twice in the Lord's Prayer, the disciples were exhorted to "pray in" the coming kingdom: "Thy kingdom come, Thy will be done" (Matt. 6:10 KJV) and "For Thine is the kingdom and the power, and the glory" (Matt. 6:13 KJV). The ultimate goal of prayer is to see the kingdom of this world transformed into the kingdom of our Lord and of His Christ (Rev. 11:15).

Focusing first on the kingdom of God addresses the thoughts and intents of our innermost motives. Whose kingdom are we building anyway? God's or ours? James addressed the issue of motivation and unanswered prayer this way:

> You ask and do not receive, because you ask amiss, that you may spend *it* on your pleasures. (James 4:3 NKJV)

God promises to supply all of our needs (Phil. 4:19), but meeting our desires and wants is secondary in importance.

Praying for the coming kingdom is our opportunity to pray for those items that are foremost on God's heart. Chapter 11 will aid you toward that end.

Prayer that moves mountains is ultimately focused on the kingdom.

5. Conveyed from the Heart

Effective prayer reflects who we really are inside. Merely reciting a prayer from a book without lending our true thoughts and feelings is akin to playing a tape of prerecorded prayers. For this reason Jesus urged His disciples against praying with vain repetition (Matt. 6:7).

The Bible was written in the common language of the people. Psalms, the original prayer book, reflects the most heartfelt and transparent emotions of its various writers. What makes the Psalms profound is not its sophisticated language, but the fact that it communicates what is common among every class of people.

The New Testament was written in *Koine* Greek, the language of the common people, not classical Greek used by the aristocracy and writers of that time. So why do we hear so many prayers offered in church filled with language we hardly understand? True prayer isn't filled with flowery words, it is expressed from the heart. John Knox, the Scottish Reformer, got right to the point in his prayer: "Give me Scotland or I die."

Prayer that moves mountains is conveyed from the heart.

6. Empowered by the Word of God

Just as important as praying from the heart is praying the anointed, inspired, Word of God. The moment Jesus was tempted in the wilderness, He picked up His sword of the Spirit and fought Satan with the Word of God (Matt. 4; Luke 4).

If, according to Hebrews 4:12, the Word of God is "living and active," then when we pray using Scripture, the Word of God works on our behalf—*even after we are finished praying!*—just like a nuclear reaction that keeps radiating into eternity.

Through Scripture we learn what God's will is. When our prayers come into line with His will, they are accomplished. If all God's promises—which we find in His Word—are "yes" and "amen" (2 Cor. 1:20), then we would be remiss by not beginning with them.

Prayer that moves mountains is empowered by the Word of God.

7. Asks in Jesus' Name

Prayer that moves mountains isn't hesitant to ask. The most commonly used Greek word for prayer in the Bible, *proseuche*, means literally "to wish" or "ask." However, it doesn't mean "to demand." Paul wrote in Philippians 4:6, "Do not be anxious about anything, but in everything, by prayer and petition, with thanksgiving, present your requests to God" (NIV). Through prayer we are given opportunity to present our requests to God.

Notice in this same verse that we are encouraged to bring anything and everything before the throne. There is no request too small or too great that God isn't willing to answer.

When we ask, we ask in Jesus' name. We don't have to implore the great saints of the past or even Mary, the mother of Jesus, to go before the Father on our behalf. Jesus is our advocate before the Father. Jesus said, "until now you have asked nothing *in My name.* Ask, and you will receive, that your joy may be full" (John 16:24 NKJV, italics added).

Prayer that moves mountains asks in Jesus' name.

8. Prays with Faith

Without faith, it is impossible for us to please God (Heb. 11:6). We must believe not only that God has the power to move our mountains through prayer, but we must also believe He has made His power available to us and that He desires to do it!

John Calvin once said, "The principal work of the Spirit is faith . . . the principal exercise of faith is prayer."[1] The main ingredient in mountain-moving prayer is faith. Let's look at what Jesus said about mountains in Mark 11:22–24:

> Have *faith* in God. For assuredly, I say to you, whoever says to this mountain, "Be removed and be cast into the sea," and does not doubt in his heart, but *believes* that those things he says will

come to pass, he will have whatever he says. Therefore I say to you, whatever things you ask when you pray, *believe* that you receive *them*, and you will have *them*. (NKJV, italics added)

Notice how often the words *faith* and *believe* are used. Faith isn't something we muster up on our own, it is nurtured through God's Word and in prayer. "So then faith comes by hearing, and hearing by the word of God" (Rom. 10:17 NKJV).

Here's how the cycle of prayer and faith works: We give ourselves to God in prayer; we grow deeper in our relationship with Him; we know better what are the issues on His heart; we see clearer what His desires are for us; we pray for them; our prayers are answered because they line up with His will; God builds more faith in our lives. And the more faith God builds in our lives, the more inclined we are to spend time with Him. As we spend more time with Him, the cycle repeats.

Prayer that moves mountains prays with faith.

9. Borne out of a Relationship

Jesus said in John 15:7, "If you remain in me and my words remain in you, ask whatever you wish, and it will be given you" (NIV). An important key to answered prayer lies in remaining in Christ—to seek Him, wait for Him, listen to Him, and allow Him to guide your prayers. Remaining in Christ implies a prior relationship.

Every salesperson worth his salt knows that the hardest sell is the cold call. But when the salesperson is able to establish a relationship with the client, the likelihood of a sale greatly increases—partially because a relationship of trust is established, but also because the seller is able to sell according to the client's needs.

The same is true in our walk with God. Asking God to answer our prayer when we have had little or nothing to do with Him beforehand is like going on a cold call. A mutual relationship of trust hasn't been established, and we are completely unaware of what the issues on His heart are.

Every relationship is based on a mutual give and take. All too often we call out to God, "Oh God, please give me direction for the future," and yet we give Him no room to speak to us. Once we've had our say, we get up off our knees and go along our way. It's no wonder so many people find their prayers going unanswered and have no sense of God's direction!

Although there is some question concerning its meaning, many Bible scholars believe the word *selah*, frequently mentioned in the Psalms (Psalm 3, for example), refers to a pause for reflection and waiting upon God.

We should all expect somewhere along the way to receive divine direction. In Scripture, *not* hearing from God was a sign of the removal of God's blessing (2 Chron. 7:14). But somewhere in the midst of the dialogue between God and us, mountain-moving prayer happens.

Prayer that moves mountains is borne out of a relationship.

10. Refuses to Give Up

Wedded to our faith we must add perseverance. Hebrews 11:6 says, "But without faith it is impossible to please Him, for he who comes to God must believe that He is, and that He is a rewarder of those who diligently seek Him."

Prayer is more a marathon than a sprint. All long-distance runners know that at some point in their run they will "hit the wall" when their will is tested. Everything within their mortal body screams to give up, but they know they must continue if they want to finish the race and win the prize.

Answers are rarely won in the first ten minutes of prayer. But as we cling to God's promises with a tenacious grip when we "hit the wall," He will either answer our prayer or change it to conform to His will. All too often, however, we give up right at the point we should really begin pressing in.

In an instant society that expects speedier computers, quicker meals, and fast-paced television programming, this essential requirement of prayer has been lost. If a prayer request isn't answered immediately, we lose interest and move on.

Jesus told the story of a widow who sought justice from an unrighteous judge. She pestered Him repeatedly until He finally gave in and answered her request. Jesus concluded the parable with these words:

> And the Lord said, "Listen to what the unjust judge says. And will not God bring about justice for his chosen ones, who cry out to him day and night? Will he keep putting them off? I tell you, he will see that they get justice, and quickly. However, when the Son of Man comes, will he find faith on the earth?" (Luke 18:6–8 NIV)

The good news is, our God is not an unjust judge! He desires to bless His children with good things! If we serve a God who is good, how much more will He answer us when we pray relentlessly? Once again, we also see the relationship between faith and perseverance. Perseverance is faith in action.

Prayer that moves mountains refuses to give up.

NOTES

Introduction

1. E. M. Bounds, *The Complete Works of E. M. Bounds on Prayer* (Grand Rapids: Baker Book House, 1990), 13.
2. Ibid, 322.

Chapter 1

1. Morton H. Smith, *Shorter Catechism of the Westminster Confession Standards* (Simpsonville, SC: Christian Classics Foundation, 1997).

Chapter 3

1. Watchman Nee, *The Prayer Ministry of the Church* (Anaheim, CA: Living Stream Ministry, 1995), 17.

Appendix

1. John Calvin, "Principal Practice of Faith," *Christian History Magazine*, Issue 12, (Carol Stream, IL: Christianity Today, Inc, 1997).

If you are interested in receiving more information about the ministry of *Prayers To Move Your Mountains,* or to host a Prayers To Move Your Mountains conference at your church, please visit out web site, www.howtopray.com.

Printed in the USA
CPSIA information can be obtained
at www.ICGtesting.com
LVHW040341151024
793772LV00012B/594

9 780785 286523